With thanks to all those who added so much to this book.

Special thanks to Drs. R. K. and S.B.K.

And true thanks to the One to whom all thanks is due.

JESUS: MYTHS & MESSAGE

Lisa Spray

UNIVERSAL UNITY
Fremont, California

Copyright © 1992 by Lisa Spray

All rights reserved
including the right of reproductions
in whole or in part in any form
Published by Universal Unity
P.O. Box 15067
Fremont, CA 94539

ISBN 1-881893-00-6

Printed in the United States of America

TABLE OF CONTENTS

	Introduction	vii
1.	Faith In Crisis	1
2.	Garbled Transmission?	6
3.	Was Jesus God?	22
4.	Where Did the Concept Come From?	50
5.	Was He the Son?	65
6.	The Trinity: Fact or Fiction?	78
7.	Sacrificial Lamb of God?	87
8.	Who Is God?	96
9.	Jesus: Search for the Proven History	109
10.	The Physical Evidence	116
11.	Virgin Birth	126
12.	Jesus' Miracles	137
13.	Jesus' Death	150
14.	Jesus' Resurrection	162
15.	Who Was Jesus?	172
16.	Epilogue to Jesus' Teachings	178
	Appendix	195
	References	203
	Index	206

INTRODUCTION

Most people growing up in the West have a pretty definite idea of who Jesus Christ was and what he taught. Jesus of Nazareth was born of a virgin, grew up in Palestine and spent the later years of his rather short life teaching of the coming of the Kingdom of God. He began a new religion which was to become one of the driving forces in Western civilization. For those who worship him, he is the son of God, part of the Godhead, or God Himself. To millions of people, this is the truth.

But is it? Well, partially. Many of the major tenets of Christianity developed centuries after the death of Christ. Some of them are contrary to his actual teachings. We will examine some of these using the Bible itself as our main reference. Then we will look at some revolutionary new developments in scriptural study. This new information is so comprehensive and conclusive that it offers us a new yardstick for evaluating and comparing traditional Christian understanding.

This is a big claim, and will necessarily be received with healthy skepticism, as any such claim should be. As detailed in Chapters 9 and 10, this evidence is an extremely intricate, computer decoded numerical structure which was discovered pervading ancient documents. The vastness and intricacy of this numerical structure is clearly super-human.

The first known report of this comprehensive mathematical coding was presented more than 900 years ago by a Hasidic Jewish rabbi, Judah the Pious. He put forth the theory "that the words and letters of the scripture are not accidental, but their order, and especially their numbers, reflect a mystical harmony. " Recent developments expand and demonstrate his theory to the extent that many researchers consider them to be proof not only of Judah the Pious' theory, but of the existence of God as well.

The references in this book cover a wide range of documents, including the Torah, the Old Testament, the New Testament, the Nag Hammadi Library, the Dead Sea Scrolls, numerous pieces of Apocryphal Christian literature, and the Quran, as well as the views of numerous Christian scholars.

Unless otherwise specified, the biblical quotes are from *THE NEW AMERICAN BIBLE, Translated from the Original Languages with Critical Use of All the Ancient Sources,* Catholic Biblical Association of America, Catholic Press, 1970. Sometimes known as the Catholic Bible, this version was chosen only because it is readily available and, unlike the King James version, it is translated from the oldest available sources rather than from previous biblical translations.

Most of the Quranic quotations are taken from *QURAN: THE FINAL TESTAMENT, Authorized English Version, Translated from the Original Arabic*, translated by Rashad Khalifa, Islamic Productions, 1989. Several quotations were translated by him specifically for this book before his manuscript had been published.

The truths which Jesus taught are an integral and critical part of human spiritual development, and of the development of Western civilization in general. Those who truly wish to follow the religion of this man, and wish to worship God as he taught, will find many questions raised, and, I hope, many more answered in this volume.

Lisa Spray
June, 1992

Chapter One

FAITH IN CRISIS

The Need For Re-examination

We live in a time of great change.

Our individual lives are often in great flux. Many people find themselves changing jobs, moving from one place to another, often from one profession to another. Even the nuclear family is unstable. The divorce rate is astounding—in 1990, almost half that of new marriages. Family ties no longer have the strength of former times.

This great instability is reflected in our society. The old patterns are breaking down, and great political and social change is taking place. On the one hand, communism is rapidly dissolving in the face of growing economic and social pressure. On the other hand, democratic societies face a myriad of seemingly overwhelming problems. There is an onslaught of violent crime, growing drug problems, increasing homelessness, spiraling environmental contamination, unrest in our inner cities, and epidemics of 'modern' diseases—most notably AIDS and cancer.

The depths of these problems is difficult to comprehend. In the United States alone, up to 3 million people are homeless on any given night. Unemployment among certain segments of our population is 25%. In May of 1992 our major cities erupted once again in violent response to social conditions. Sparked by the decision in the Rodney King case, the breadth and violence of the rioting and looting which took place in the next few days stunned the nation and the world.

The situation with AIDS is just as sobering. What we are seeing now is just the tip of the iceberg, and already by the end of 1990, in major US cities, AIDS was the main cause of death for women between the ages of 20 and 40. There are estimates of 10 to 20 million people infected with HIV, the precursor to AIDS, world wide.

These are just samples of the great problems facing our society today. We could go on reciting them for volumes. These problems, in and of themselves, force dramatic changes within the lives of individuals, and society as a whole. And that change necessitates further changes.

CHANGE WITHIN CHRISTIANITY

Churches find themselves caught in the middle of this great whirlwind of change. Uncertain how to react to the drastic modifications in needs and attitudes of their members, they themselves must respond to the issues at hand. This internal conflict is vividly expressed by L. Howard in his article in the July 15, 1991 issue of *Christianity & Crisis*. He had been present at the General Assembly of the Presbyterian Church in Baltimore when it voted on the report of its committee on human sexuality, which urged greater acceptance of homosexuals by the Church:

> What is perhaps most clear in Baltimore was that the crisis in human sexuality in our society and our churches is not limited. As the pastoral letter says, "We are being torn apart by issues of teenage sexuality and practice, sexual violence, clergy sexual misconduct, new reproductive technologies, AIDS and other sexually transmitted diseases, and the sexual needs of gay and lesbian persons, the disabled, and older adults."
>
> The report may not have been received officially. But the Presbyterian Church is forever changed by the debate it engendered.

Out of necessity, there is great change within most denominations. Views are changing regarding birth control, homosexuality, divorce and a myriad of other social and religious issues.

In response to all of this personal, social and religious upheaval, many people have found themselves re-evaluating their own faith. Some have come to reject the concept of a deity outright. Others now have serious doubts about some of the doctrines of their religion.

CURRENT PERCEPTIONS OF JESUS
At the core of those doctrines is the identity of Jesus Christ.

For most Protestant denominations, Jesus is part of the Trinity and might be defined as God's manifestation or revelation of Himself in human form.

Catholics also accept the Trinity and bestow upon Mary the title of the 'Mother of God,' thus asserting that Jesus is, for them, truly man and truly God.

Some of the more recently formed denominations have quite a different view. For instance, Jehovah's Witnesses do not accept the Trinity and see Jesus as the ransom sacrifice to redeem humanity, not God Himself. And Unitarians generally see Jesus as a great teacher and example, but fully human and God's son only in the same sense that all humans are His children.

On the scholarly front, there has long been a wide range of understandings of Jesus. He has been seen as an Essene scholar, a member of a radical Jewish political movement, a witty rabbi, and many other things. For years a number of scholars have worked to discern the historical figure of Jesus Christ from the background of the scriptural narrations and whatever other sources they could find. That interest continues today, as is witnessed by the recent paper back reprinting of Albert Schweitzer's book *The Quest of the Historical Jesus*, and the new release of John Crossan (*The Historical Jesus*, Harper Collins, 1991).

For some scholars, like John Bowden, the search has ended in serious questioning and skepticism. For others the skepticism goes farther. As an example, G. A. Wells poses the following question about Jesus: "Can we really be sure that a person described in these terms ever had any earthly existence?" His answer is summed up by the last thought in his book: "is it not time to look elsewhere than in the Scriptures for guidance in our living, and to stop basing our decisions and choices on ancient fantasies?" (*Who Was Jesus?* G. A. Wells, Open Court Publishing, La Salle, IL, 1989.)

The popular press also reflects a reassessment of our moral and religious values. Such reassessment is natural given the relatively recent surfacing of television evangelist scandals, the fresh memory of the Jonestown horror, and the realization that even Hitler used the banner of Christianity to try to help justify the abomination of genocide.

With all these factors, it seems almost imperative that thinking people re-examine their own beliefs. Thus, the writing of this book.

Such reassessment is essentially a personal task. Within this examination, a great deal can be learned from the excellent work done by many scholars. I have referred to such work often in the following pages. But the essence of faith is very personal. No one else can tell you exactly what your personal relationship should be with your Creator. You must find that for yourself.

And no one else can tell you who Jesus is for you. This is a totally personal issue, between you and God.

Christianity is a religion of great diversity. The brief inventory of different denominational views of Jesus given above and a quick perusal of the church listings in any phone book leaves no doubt of that fact. The variability in beliefs and practices is matched only by the variability of human beings.

It is not the intention of this book to address the beliefs of any specific denomination. Nor is it the intent to attack any of them, nor Christianity as a whole.

Rather, in this first portion of the book, I hope to give you some insight into certain Christian beliefs in relation to the teachings of Christ as they are recorded in the scriptures. Later in the book I hope to introduce some new information that you may find useful in the assessment of your own beliefs.

My hope in doing this is that you will find your own personal way to go about following the most important commandment for all humanity, the commandment which Jesus himself called the Great Commandment:

> *You shall worship God with all your heart,*
> *and all your soul, and all your mind*
> *and all your strength.*

[Deuteronomy 6:5, Matthew 22:37, Mark 12:30 and Luke 10:27]

Chapter Two

GARBLED TRANSMISSION?

Role of the Scripture Writers and Translators

> At first, Christians gave little thought to their own history. The Lord would return soon, they believed, and put an end to all history. When men give up their jobs, gaze into the heavens, and look for the end of the world, they write no history. Why record the past if there will be no one to remember it?
>
> —Robert Wilken
> (*Myth of Christian Beginnings*, 1971)

We tend to think of the early Christians as pious men who knew that they were helping to form and spread a religion which would become the great force that it is today. We assume that the disciples Matthew, Mark, Luke and John wrote the Gospels as tools to be used in the early spread of that religion. It comes as a surprise to most people that the first writings to circulate among early Christians were Paul's letters.

In face, much of what we recognize today as the basic teachings of Christianity came to us through Paul, originally known as Saul of Tarsus. Though he never met Jesus, he was the major missionary to the gentiles in the years immediately following the crucifixion.

His letters were written to various different congregations, often trying to solve localized problems, or to consolidate the faithful into one cohesive congregation, rather than to document and spread the teachings of Jesus. For the early Christians, the Kingdom of God was very close at hand. They expected it at any time. These expectations undoubtedly changed the nature of the transmission of Jesus' teachings.

Any study of Christian doctrines must deal with the issues involved in that transmission, for it is only through the transmission process that we have any idea what Jesus taught.

TEACHINGS COME SECONDHAND

Frank W. Beare in the Introduction of his book *THE EARLIEST RECORDS OF JESUS* (Abingdon Press, 1962, pp. 16, 18) gives us a glimpse of the problems faced right from the beginning by anybody researching in the field:

> In any serious study of the Gospels, we have always to keep in mind that Jesus himself left nothing in writing, and that the earliest records of his career which have come down to us were not put into writing until about forty years after his death. All our knowledge of him is drawn from the deposit of a tradition which was transmitted for several decades by word of mouth. We are therefore obliged to raise the question of the relationship between the documents as we have them and the events and sayings which they report. For it must be realized that in a generation or more of oral transmission, sayings and stories do not remain unchanged. Once they have been committed to writing, they are to some degree stabilized, as it were; though even at this stage, we have to observe that Luke and Matthew do not shrink from altering the Marcan record which they are both using....

> We cannot too lightly assume that what the earliest Christians thought worth preserving would be identical with what we ourselves would regard as most important, or even that it would reflect essentially what Jesus himself regarded as central to his message. It must be regarded as possible that 'Jesus was over the heads of his reporters,' and we shall indeed find indications in the Gospels themselves that he from time to time manifested keen disappointment and even a certain impatience with the lack of understanding shown by his immediate disciples...it is not at all unlikely that the...people who followed him may not have been capable of taking in all the range of his thought, and communicating it clearly to others.

Beare's first point is that sayings and stories change as they are passed by word of mouth from person to person and generation to generation. To illustrate, do you remember the children's game "Telephone"? Everyone sits in a circle and one person whispers something into the ear of the next person. The message is passed from ear to ear until it comes back to the person who first whispered it. By the time it gets back to the original source, it is totally different from the original message, causing much amazement and laughter.

We know from the above short history of the Gospels that most, if not all, of the initial transmission was oral, and that the Gospels were not written down until several years (perhaps as many as forty or fifty years for the earliest—the Gospel of Matthew) had passed after Jesus' departure. In that period of time, many human errors could have entered the transmission, and indeed did.

To make things more difficult, there are variations among ancient manuscripts of the same material. Sometimes these variations are minor, but sometimes they are substantial. Thus, even committing the transmission to writing did not solve all the problems.

Beare's second point is that we do not know that the apostles always understood Jesus and correctly and clearly transmitted his teachings. To expand that, the process of attempting to communicate clearly to others did not stop with the initial writing of the gospels. The revising and 'clarifying' continues even to this day. On almost every page of any annotated English version of the New Testament, there are variant readings from ancient texts for one or more verses.

Once the Gospels were committed to writing, they were still fragmented and difficult to come by, as the following quote from Dr. George Lamsa demonstrates (*NEW TESTAMENT ORIGIN*, Aramaic Bible Society, Inc., no date given, p.65):

> Even today in Turkey and Persia complete manuscripts of the Scriptures are very rare. Scrolls containing portions of the Bible are found in the possession of various families. In some districts one portion may be found in one village and the other completing portions perhaps in towns many miles away. When family ties are broken, the scrolls or

books are divided among the members. The student of the Bible must remember that in Jesus' day libraries, printing presses, and paper were unknown and that sacred writings were available only to the priests, rich men, and rulers.

This continued unavailability of written scripture would have caused oral transmission to be an important factor in the developing doctrines and attitudes of Christianity, even after the Gospels were recorded. This fact may also help explain some of the differences among manuscripts.

In any case, it is certain that there is a great variability among manuscripts of the Gospels.

AUTHENTICITY NEVER KNOWN

With so much variation among manuscripts, the absolute authenticity of any text, even the most venerable manuscripts, is always in question. The Codex Vaticanus is a prime example of this. The facsimile reproductions edited by the Vatican City in 1965 include an accompanying editorial note with the following information:

> Several centuries after it was copied, a scribe inked over all the letters except those he thought were a mistake.... The different hands that corrected and annotated the manuscript over the centuries have not yet been definitely discerned; a certain number of corrections were undoubtedly made when the text was inked over.

Sir Frederic Kenyon lists some of the important variations in the manuscripts of the Gospels (*OUR BIBLE AND THE ANCIENT MANUSCRIPTS*, Harper and Brothers, 1958, pp. 48-49):

> The Doxology of the Lord's Prayer is omitted in the oldest copies of Matt. vi. 13; several copies omit Matt. xvi. 2, 3 altogether; a long additional passage is sometimes found after Matt. xx 28; the last twelve verses of St. Mark are omitted altogether by the two oldest copies of the original Greek; one very ancient authority inserts an additional incident after Luke vi. 4, while it alters the account of the institution of the Lord's Supper in Luke xxii. 19, 20, and omits altogether Peter's visit to the sepulcher in xxiv. 12, and several other details of the Resurrection; the version of the Lord's Prayer in Luke xi. 2-4 is much

abbreviated in many copies; the incident of the Bloody Sweat is omitted in xxii. 43, 44, as also is the word from the Cross, "Father, forgive them", in xxiii. 34; the mention of the descent of an angel to cause the moving of the waters of Bethesda is entirely absent from the oldest copies of John v. 4, and all the best authorities omit the incident of the woman taken in adultery in vii. 53-viii. 11. Besides the larger discrepancies, such as these, there is scarcely a verse in which there is not some variation of phrase in some copies. No one can say that these additions or omissions or alterations are matters of mere indifference.

These variations and possible distortions are not "matters of mere indifference" because many Christian beliefs are based on a small portion of the Bible. If those portions have been distorted or misunderstood, then the beliefs themselves may actually go against the teachings of Jesus.

If we are trying to worship God with all our heart, all our mind, all our soul, and all our strength, then some traditional Christian beliefs may be getting in our way, without our even being aware of it.

HUMAN ERRORS

Why are there so many variations in the manuscripts? As one possible answer, Kenyon goes on to describe the types of errors introduced into manuscripts of the Gospels by the copyists. He divides them into three basic types. The first type of error has to do with the mechanics of hand copying long documents. Words with similar sounds or spellings are easily confused, letters and words can easily be skipped and abbreviations or contractions can be misunderstood. We must remember that hand copying, unlike touch typing, requires constant looking from the original to the new copy. When the same words are used in different lines, the copyist may pick up again at the wrong occurrence of the words, thus omitting intervening text.

Given the fact that there were no spaces between words, little punctuation, and no difference between capital and lower case letters in ancient manuscripts, it is easy to see how marginal notes might have been mistaken for part of the scripture, and included as such. Poor lighting, adverse working conditions and poor nutrition undoubtedly plagued the copyists, making their task more difficult and prone to error.

Kenyon describes a second type of error that he calls 'Errors of the Mind.' This is the intentional or unintentional harmonizing of two similar passages. This happens especially easily when two passages contain the same words, but in a different order. If one is more familiar with one order, it is easy to use that order on both passages without even realizing one is doing so.

The final type of textual alteration that Kenyon discusses is the deliberate type. These are the most dangerous, and most likely to affect doctrinal issues.

In spite of Kenyon's assertion that none of the fundamental Christian doctrines is dependent on a disputed reading, he states (Ibid p. 52):

> At times reverential and dogmatic motives have influenced the transmission of the text. Thus, e.g., the incident of the ministering Angel and the Bloody Sweat in Gethsemane, Luke xxii:43-44, is omitted by a number of MSS (including Vaticanus) and representatives of the version because, it might seem, these verses were inconsistent with the divinity of Christ.

Clearly, in some cases, important doctrines are affected by disputed readings.

Then, not only were the original documents subject to corruption in copying, but there were also the inevitable changes introduced as they were translated from language to language. Every person working on a translation, or the revision of one, naturally introduces changes as they try to make it more correct or clearer. The changes introduced depend on that person's body of knowledge, viewpoint and grasp of the languages involved.

KING JAMES AS A CASE IN POINT

There are always major difficulties in translating from one language to another. Often idioms and even individual words are colored by the culture which produced them. This makes direct translation impossible, and unless the translator is very familiar with the cultural context, the attempted translation may be far from the original flavor and intent. Communicating Hebrew/Aramaic ideas and outlook in such a culturally alien language as Greek poses special problems, of which the early translators may not have always been aware. All of these problems are compounded when translations are again translated, as was the case for the gospels.

The majority of English speaking Protestants use the King James translation in one of its many revisions. It is often considered the standard translation. George Lamsa has a nice look at the history of the King James version in the introduction to his own 1957 translation of the Bible (*THE HOLY BIBLE, FROM ANCIENT EASTERN MANUSCRIPTS.* A.J. Holman Co, 1957):

> When the King James translation was made, western scholars had no access to the East as we have today. In the 16th century, A.D., the Turkish empire had extended its borders as far as Vienna...the Scriptures in Aramaic were unknown in Europe. The only resource scholars had was to Latin and to a few portions of Greek manuscripts.... It is a miracle that the King James' translators were able to produce such a remarkable translation from sources available in this dark period of European history. Even fifty years ago, the knowledge of Western scholars relative to the Eastern Scriptures in Aramaic and the Christian Church in the East was conjectural. Moreover, these scholars knew very little of the Eastern customs and manners in which the Biblical literature was nurtured.

All of these factors have led to some definite problems in the translation. Johannes Lehmann gives a very good example of the lack of understanding that can occur in trying to translate from culturally different languages. (See his *Rabbi J.* Stein and Day, New York, 1971.) He refers to the following verse:

On the third day there was a wedding at Canna in Galilee,
and the mother of Jesus was there.

[John 2:1]

What is this third day? The third day after what? Some translators have omitted the reference to the day at all, others have tried to make it the third day after the wedding. But there is a very simple explanation. Except for the Sabbath, Jewish days do not have names. They are numbered from the Sabbath. Thus the third day is our Tuesday.

In the above example, the effect of the translation is unimportant. But in some cases, the whole meaning of the passage has been changed. Lamsa cites a good example of the dramatic reversal of meaning:

> In the King James version, we read in Numbers 25:4:
> "And the Lord said unto Moses, 'Take all the heads of the people, and hang them up before the Lord against the sun, that the fierce anger of the Lord may be turned away from Israel.'"
>
> The Aramaic reads:
> "And the Lord said unto Moses, 'Take all the chiefs of the people and expose them before the Lord in the daylight that the fierce anger of the Lord may be turned away from the children of Israel.'"

The difference between exposing the corruption of a group's chiefs, and hanging them or their heads before God is quite dramatic.

There is yet another example of dramatic translational distortion in the King James version. This time it has contributed to the doctrine of the divinity of Jesus. It has to do with the crucial word *worship*. Here is the King James version of Matthew 2:1-2 and 2:7-8:

> *Now when Jesus was born in Beth-lehem of Judaea*
> *in the days of Herod the King, behold, there came*
> *wise men from the East to Jerusalem, saying,*
> *Where is he that is born king of the Jews?*
> *for we have seen his star in the east,*
> *and are come to* **worship** *him.*
> **[Matthew 2:1-2]**

> *Then Herod, when he had privily called the wise men,*
> *enquired of them diligently what time the star appeared.*
> *And he sent them to Beth-lehem, and said,*
> *Go and search diligently for the young child;*
> *and when ye have found him,*

*bring me word again,
that I may come and **worship** him also.*
         [Matthew 2:7-8]

Let us now compare these same verses as translated in the *NEW AMERICAN BIBLE*, which is a recent translation drawing from the oldest documents available to the translators, rather than being a revision of earlier translations as the King James version is:

*After Jesus' birth in Bethlehem of Judea
during the reign of King Herod,
astrologers from the east arrived one day in Jerusalem
inquiring, "Where is the newborn king of the Jews?
We observed his star at its rising and have come
to **pay him homage**."*
         [Matthew 2:1-2]

*Herod called the astrologers aside and found out
from them the exact time of the star's appearance.
Then he sent them to Bethlehem, after having instructed
them: "Go and get detailed information about the child.
When you have found him, report your findings to me
so that I may go and **offer him homage** too."*
         [Matthew 2:7-8]

Notice that the King James version tells us that the Magi and Herod spoke of *'worshiping'* the Christ child, while the New American Bible says they wanted to *'pay homage'* to him. How do we know that *"pay homage"* is more correct than *"worship,"* or vice versa?

First, we know that in general the New American Bible is a more current and scholarly translation than the King James version. This is not to belittle the effort put into the King James version, but to simply reiterate Lamsa's point that there have been great strides in Bible scholarship in the four centuries which have passed since it was produced.

Furthermore, it makes more sense that Herod would say he wished to pay homage to the one he calls *"king of the Jews,"* rather than wanting to worship him. Homage is due to a king; worship is due to one you consider divine.

TRANSLATION OF 'WORSHIP' AS AN EXAMPLE

The human tendency is to introduce one's own understanding into a translation. This constitutes a major pitfall in any translation, but in scriptural translation it has wide-ranging consequences, since it affects the religious doctrine upheld by millions of people.

There is another example of this translation error found in both the King James and *NEW AMERICAN BIBLE* versions of John 9:38.

*When Jesus heard of his expulsion, he sought him out
and asked him, "Do you believe in the Son of Man?"
He answered, "Who is he, sir, that I may believe in him?"
"You have seen him," Jesus replied.
"He is speaking to you now."
"I do believe, Lord," he said,
and he bowed down to **worship** him.*
[John 9:35-38]

An authority on the Bible and its original language, George Lamsa, explains the crucial word *"worship"* as it occurs specifically here in John 9:38. In his book *GOSPEL LIGHT* (1936 edition, p. 353), Lamsa writes:

> The Aramaic word **sagad,** worship, also means to bend or to kneel down. Easterners in greeting each other generally bow the head or bend down. When a ruler or holy man is greeted, the people kneel before him. "He worshipped him" does not imply that he worshipped Jesus as one who worshipped God. Such an act would have been regarded as sacrilegious and a breach of the first commandment in the eyes of the Jews and the man might have been stoned. But he knelt before him in token of homage and gratitude. This is also a sign of self-surrender and loyalty. The blind man worshipped Jesus in acknowledgment of his divine power and in appreciation of his compassion on him in opening his eyes. He had no knowledge of the claims of

16   JESUS: MYTHS & MESSAGE

Jesus nor was he interested in his teachings, but he was convinced by the miracle performed that he must be a holy man and one empowered by God.

It is noteworthy that, in addition to the translation error discussed above, a footnote in the *NEW AMERICAN BIBLE* points out another problem with this verse:

> 9:38 This verse, omitted in important MSS, may be an addition for a baptismal liturgy.

In other words, John 9:38, stating that the man *"bowed down to worship Jesus"* was probably added to the scriptural text. The indication is that it was added as part of the passage's use in the liturgy used for a baptism.

EXAMPLE OF 'RACIAL' BIAS

There are many other instances of human introduced bias throughout the Bible. In Genesis, for example, there is a clear illustration of 'racial' bias as shown in these verses from the King James version:

> *And Hagar bare Abram a son: and Abram called his son's*
> *name, which Hagar bare, Ishmael.*
> *And Abram was fourscore and six years old,*
> *when Hagar bare Ishmael to Abram.*
>   **[Genesis 16:15-16]**

> *For Sarah conceived, and bare Abraham a son*
> *in his old age, at the set time of which God*
> *had spoken to him.*
> *And Abraham called the name*
> *of his son that was born unto him,*
> *whom Sarah bare to him, Isaac.*
> *And Abraham circumcised his son Isaac*
> *being eight days old, as God had commanded him.*
> *And Abraham was an hundred years old*
> *when his son Isaac was born unto him.*
>   **[Genesis 21:2-5]**

This means that Ishmael was fourteen years old when Isaac was born.

*And it came to pass after these things,
that God did tempt Abraham,
and said unto him, Abraham:
and he said, Behold, here I am.
And he said, Take now thy son,
thine only son Isaac, whom thou lovest,
and get thee unto the land of Moriah;
and offer him there for a burnt offering
upon one of the mountains
which I will tell thee of.*
[Genesis 22:1-2]

But we know that Isaac was never the only son of Abraham; Ishmael was Abraham's only son for 14 years until Isaac was born. Thus, we see here that the Jewish writer wanted to bestow the honor upon Isaac, his ancestor.

Some have raised the possibility that Ishmael might not be considered a son of Abraham, since his mother, Hagar, was an Egyptian slave. However, we find that the scripture has considered Ishmael to be a son of Abraham, up until Abraham's death:

*And these are the days of the years of Abraham's life
which he lived, an hundred threescore and fifteen years.
Then Abraham gave up the ghost, and died
in a good old age, an old man, and full of years:
and was gathered to his people.
And his sons Isaac and Ishmael buried him
in the cave of Machpelah....*
[Genesis 25:7-9]

The above illustration, though it is not from the New Testament, shows how easily human prejudices can enter into the scripture and become accepted as the truth, even when they are contradictory. This is very important for us to examine. While we certainly do not want to discard the Bible, with all its great wisdom and comfort, we must be aware of the ways in which it may have been changed.

HISTORY OF THE GOSPELS

A review of the general history of the Gospels may help us understand the inconsistencies we observe.

As mentioned before, it comes as a surprise to most people that the first religious writings of the early Christians were Paul's letters. These letters occupied a prevalent position long before the Gospels. It was not until late in the second century that the four Gospels were officially accepted by the Church as genuine, thus becoming part of the canon.

Each of these four canonic Gospels went through its own vicissitudes. For example, in its *"Introduction to the Books of the New Testament,"* THE NEW AMERICAN BIBLE (Ibid, p. xxxiv) notes that there were probably several Greek translations of the early collection attributed to Matthew. The introduction to the Gospel according to John is even more telling:

> ...It should be remembered that for the ancients authorship was a much broader concept than it is today. In their time a man could be called the "author" of a work if he was the authority behind it, even though he did not write it. Modern critical analysis makes it difficult to accept that the fourth gospel as it now stands was written by one man. Chapter 21 seems to have been added after the gospel was completed; it exhibits a Greek style somewhat different from the rest of the work....Within the gospel itself there are signs of some disorder; e.g., there are two endings to Jesus' discourse at the Last Supper.
> [*NEW AMERICAN BIBLE*, p. xxxvii]

The footnote goes on to state a widely accepted theory that the Gospel of John was actually written by someone other than John, probably his disciple, and then later edited by another disciple. How much, if any, direct input actually came from John is impossible to know.

Frank Beare goes even further and declares all the gospels to be anonymous, with their traditional names being "second-century guesses."

During the period in which the church was organized there was an abundance of literature with widely divergent views of Jesus. Church officials set about deciding on the officially acceptable materials. As many as one hundred gospels were excluded, and only the four we have today were retained to make up the "Canon." Needless to say, only gospels that agreed with the Church's views at that time were canonized. This is especially significant when we recall that the Church had become a political, not just a religious, establishment during the second century.

The canonization of four Gospels, rather than just one, indicates that there were some compromises to satisfy the wide range of divergent views that must have been in the scores of gospels that existed at that time. If the church authorities had agreed on everything, we would have ended up with only one authorized Gospel, the Gospel of Jesus.

Marcion of Sinope founded a Gnostic movement around 140 A.D. He acknowledged the Gospel of Luke as the only authentic Gospel. He believed that Luke, who was almost certainly a non-Jew, was the spokesman for Paul. Marcion exerted tremendous pressure upon the ecclesiastic authorities to accept only Luke. Since he was an ardent enemy of the Jews, he rejected the whole of the Old Testament. The Church, however, declared Marcion a heretic and put in its canon all the Epistles of Paul. In addition, they included the other canonized Gospels, Luke's Acts of the Apostles, and other works.

It was not until the councils of Hippo Regius (A.D. 393) and Carthage (A.D. 397) that the contents of the New Testament were solidified. Up until that time, what was accepted by the Church as authentic scripture varied. Some works that were then excluded are now accepted as part of the New Testament, and vice versa.

For almost four centuries after Jesus, the Christian scripture was not put into any definite order. The oldest available manuscripts of the gospels date from the fourth century. Older documents (e.g., papyri from the First to Third Century) contain no more than small fragments of the gospels.

The two oldest parchment manuscripts are not even in the language of Jesus; they are in Fourth century Greek. They are the Codex Vaticanus, now preserved in the Vatican library, and the Codex Sinaiticus, which was discovered in the monastery of St. Catherine on Mount Sinai and is now preserved in the British Museum, London. This second manuscript contains two apocryphal works. The place of discovery of Codex Vaticanus is unknown.

INCONSISTENCIES LEAD TO DOUBT
Many critical readers of the Bible find borrowing, inconsistency and contradiction among the scriptures. A typical example of this general disillusionment is found in Carl Sagan's best selling novel of the 1980's, entitled *CONTACT* (Simon and Schuster, 1985, p. 30). Sagan's heroine points out serious contradictions in the New Testament which led her to question its divine inspiration:

> When they came to the New Testament, Ellie's agitation increased. Matthew and Luke traced the ancestral line of Jesus back to King David. But for Matthew there were twenty-eight generations between David and Jesus; for Luke forty-three. There were almost no names common to the two lists. How could both Matthew and Luke be the Word of God? The contradictory genealogies seemed to Ellie a transparent attempt to fit the Isianic prophecy after the event — cooking the data, it was called in chemistry lab.

The problem of Jesus' genealogy and its inconsistencies was also evidently noted by the scribe working on the fifth or sixth century Codex Bezae, now in the Cambridge University Library. This enterprising cleric put Matthew's genealogy into Luke, padding it where necessary!

With such discrepancies among manuscripts of the Gospels, and among the accepted Gospels themselves, it is impossible to decide which versions are the closest to the original truth. Perhaps in the future, discoveries of new manuscripts will give us a closer approximation.

CONCLUSION
In summary, we have discussed several sources of error in the Bible as it exists today:
1. The natural changes that take place over an extended period of oral transmission;

2. Errors in the original transmission due to the lack of understanding of Jesus' intent;

3. Copying errors resulting from the tedious process of hand copying, which was the only means of reproduction for the centuries before the invention of the printing press;

4. Translation errors resulting from the lack of understanding of linguistic rules, grammar and idioms, and of the culture;

5. Errors resulting from the translator's unconscious bias toward personal convictions, i.e., human bias;

6. Intentional innovation: conscious additions to the scripture for prejudicial, political or other reasons.

The importance of these errors lies in their effect on the basic doctrines of Christianity. As we have seen in this chapter, and will see even more clearly in future chapters, verses that seem to support some of the fundamental doctrines of today's Christianity may well be mistranslated or taken out of their cultural and temporal context, thus giving a distorted picture of the original teachings of Jesus.

This may be discouraging to searching Christians. It should not be. Though humans may have introduced distortion, none of this possible distortion affects the fact that two thousand years ago a man walked on earth, delivering a message of hope and strength. He spoke of the coming Kingdom of God, and how to gain admission to it. He taught us how to love and worship God with our whole beings, and thus win the prize of redemption.

No human interference can ever change the essential truth of Christ's message, but clearly decerning it from our human concepts may seem almost impossible. A look at some of the basic doctrines of Christianity may help clarify the issue.

Chapter Three

WAS JESUS GOD?

At one time or another we have all asked ourselves: Who is God? Having been raised in a Christian society I had been told that Jesus was God. I wasn't certain. Was Jesus God?

Who *was* Jesus?

In trying to answer this question we will be drawing on many sources of information, a few of which most Christians have not explored.

Again, our goal with this book is simply to try to come closer to God. To do that we must internalize Christ's teaching to "love the Lord your God with all your heart, all your soul, all your mind, and all your strength" (Mark 12:30 & Luke 10:27).

Back to our question: Was Jesus God? The answer may come as a shock to many Christians, as it did to me. Jesus never said he was God. Actually, he said over and over, and in many ways, that he was not God.

Jesus was a practicing Jew, and such a concept is now, and would have been then, totally against the law of Moses (Mosaic law).

JESUS FOLLOWED MOSAIC LAW
The next few quotes from the Bible show us that Jesus was a devout and learned Jew, a rabbi:

*Jesus returned in the power of the Spirit to Galilee,
and his reputation spread throughout the region.
He was teaching in their synagogues,*

and all were loud in his praise.
He came to Nazareth where he had been reared,
and entering the synagogue on the sabbath as he was
in the habit of doing, he stood up to do the reading.
                    [Luke 4:14-16]

The worship of God was always focal in his life, even as a child. The second chapter of Luke tells us a very touching story of Jesus as a precociously wise child of twelve, sitting for days among the scholars. His family had accidentally left him in Jerusalem after their annual visit for the Passover. Nearly frantic, they searched for him:

On the third day they came upon him in the temple sitting
in the midst of the teachers, listening to them and asking
them questions. All who heard him were amazed at his
intelligence and his answers. When his parents saw him
they were astonished, and his mother said to him:
"Son, why have you done this to us? You see that
your father and I have been searching for you in sorrow."
He said to them: "Why did you search for me?
Did you not know I had to be in my Father's house?"
                    [Luke 2:46-49]

As he grew, *"Jesus...progressed steadily in wisdom and age and grace before God and men"* (Luke 2:52). After he had matured, his opinion was sought, though perhaps not always respectfully, by traditional Jews. An example of this is John's narration of the adulterous woman brought to Jesus for judgment.

Though they addressed him as *"Teacher,"* they tried to trap him into saying something which they could use against him. As he straightened up from where he had been writing on the ground, he issued his famous judgement: *"Let him without sin cast the first stone."* Though they had come to trap him, the scribes and Pharisees could not argue and drifted away, leaving the woman without harming her. Even those who were hostile to his teachings respected him.

OTHER SCRIPTURAL SOURCES

While religious scholars of most faiths would agree that Jesus was a wonderful model for humanity, the scriptures of almost all the major religions predate Christ, and therefore give us no new information about him. The one exception to this is the Quran, the scripture of Islam.

Unfortunately, what the world recognizes as the religion of Islam is really the cultural tradition of the Muslim world. Most Muslims have not studied the Quran, and they do not really follow it. Comparing what they do in the name of Islam with the teachings of the Quran is like comparing the Spanish Inquisition with the teachings of the Bible. The practice is almost in total opposition to the scripture.

The basic message of the Quran and the Bible are the same. If we look at just the Quran itself, and leave the culture and tradition behind, we find a great deal of valuable information about Jesus and what he taught.

According to the Quran, not only was Jesus a young scholar, but he was a prophet from birth, delivering divine revelations, even shortly after birth :

She came with him to her family, carrying him.
They said, "O Mary,
you have committed something gross.
O descendant of Aaron, your father was not a bad man,
nor was your mother unchaste."
She pointed to him.
They said, "How can we talk with an infant in the crib?"
(The infant spoke and) said, "I am a servant of God.
He has given me the scripture, and made me a prophet.
He made me blessed wherever I go, and enjoined me
to observe the contact prayers (Salat) and the obligatory
charity (Zakat) for as long as I live. I am to obey
my mother; He did not make me a disobedient rebel.
And peace be upon me the day I was born, the day I die,
and the day I get resurrected."
Such was Jesus, the son of Mary.

*This is the truth of this matter,
about which they have a lot of doubt.*
[Quran 19:27-34]

We see from this and the following quote that Jesus taught even as a newborn infant.

*(On the Day of Resurrection) God will say, "O Jesus,
son of Mary, remember My blessings upon you and
your mother. I supported you with the Holy Spirit;
you thus spoke to the people from the crib,
as well as an adult..."*
[Quran 5:110]

In the above verse, it is useful to understand the Quranic definition of the Holy Spirit as the angel who brings divine revelation from God, the angel Gabriel. The Quran teaches that Gabriel brought the revelation from God to Jesus, who then delivered it to the people, and this process began even while Jesus was an infant.

This Quranic concept of revelation from God is fully supported by the first two verses in the biblical Book of Revelation:

*This is the revelation God gave to Jesus Christ, that
he might show his servants what must happen very soon.
He made it known by sending his angel to his servant John,
who in reporting all he saw bears witness
to the word of God and the testimony of Jesus Christ.*
[Revelation 1:1-2]

BASIC TEACHINGS

As a rabbi, what did Jesus teach? Throughout the New Testament, Jesus exhorted us to worship God alone and keep the Mosaic commandments. The first and best known commandment in both the Old Testament and the New Testament advocates total and absolute devotion to God alone:

*The Lord our God is Lord **alone**!
Therefore, you shall adore the Lord your God
with all your heart,*

with all your soul,
with all your mind,
and with all your strength.
                [Deuteronomy 6:4-5]
                [Mark 12:29-30]

Jesus especially stressed this First Commandment:
The scribe said to him: "Excellent, Teacher!
You are right in saying, 'He is the One,
there is no other than He.'
Yes, 'to love him with all our heart, with all our thoughts
and with all our strength,
and to love our neighbor as ourselves' is worth more
than any burnt offering or sacrifice."
Jesus approved the insight of his answer and told him,
"You are not far from the reign of God."
                [Mark 12:32-34]

THE GREAT COMMANDMENT

Again, Jesus' straightforward injunctions to follow the commandments in general, and the First Commandment in particular, are throughout the New Testament. Significantly, he described the First Commandment as "The Great Commandment" (Mark 12:29). The statement of this injunction is very strong:

I, the Lord, am your God
who brought you out of the land of Egypt,
that place of slavery.
You shall not have any other gods beside me.
You shall not carve idols for yourselves in the shape
of anything in the sky above or on the earth below
or in the waters beneath the earth;
you shall not bow down before them
or worship them.
For I, the Lord, your God, am a jealous God....
                [Deuteronomy 5:6-9]

For Jesus, this commandment meant more than just an injunction against physically worshiping idols. Often people use phrases like 'he worships the ground she walks on,' or 'he's my idol.' These phrases show the subtle idol worship that pervades our daily lives. Jesus taught the absolute devotion to God alone:

> *On one occasion a lawyer stood up to pose him this*
> *problem: "Teacher, what must I do to inherit everlasting life?"*
> *Jesus answered him: "What is written in the law?*
> *How do you read it?"*
> *He replied: "You shall love the Lord your God with all*
> *your heart, with all your soul, with all your strength,*
> *and with all your mind; and your neighbor as yourself."*
> *Jesus said: "You have answered correctly.*
> *Do this and you shall live."*
> **[Luke 10:25-28]**

If you do love God with all your heart, all your soul, all your strength and all your mind—literally with your whole being— there is not room for *anything* else. That is the definition of devotion.

Jesus taught that this devotion to God must be more than lip service:

> *"Yet an hour is coming, and is already here,*
> *when authentic worshipers will worship the Father*
> *in Spirit and truth. Indeed, it is just such worshipers the*
> *Father seeks. God is Spirit, and those who worship him*
> *must worship in Spirit and truth."*
> **[John 4:23-24]**

We see that Jesus stressed pure worship of the Father, in spirit and truth. It is not possible that Jesus could have so strongly taught total devotion to God, and then advocated his own worship.

EARLY CHRISTIAN JEWS

It is also very clear that the early Christians still considered themselves to be Jews, and thus subject to the Mosaic laws revealed in the Torah. Dr. George M. Lamsa, in his book *NEW TESTAMENT ORIGIN* (Aramaic Bible Society, Inc., p. 9), makes a point of the Jewish origins of Christianity, and his quote from Matthew stresses Jesus' adherence to Mosaic law:

> ...Christians for some time continued to worship in the Jewish temple and in the synagogues, to observe Jewish customs and traditions, and to keep the Mosaic law and the Sabbath. For nearly two centuries the bishops of Jerusalem were Semites. In other words, the followers of Jesus were loyal to the teachings of the prophets as expounded by their Master, who had told them that he had not come to destroy the law and the prophets but to fulfill them. Jesus said:
> *Think not that I am come to destroy the law, or the prophets:*
> *I am not come to destroy, but to fulfill. For verily I say unto you,*
> *till heaven and earth pass, one jot or one tittle*
> *shall in no wise pass from the law, till all be fulfilled.*
> *Whosoever therefore shall break one of these least*
> *commandments, and shall teach men so,*
> *he shall be called the least in the kingdom of heaven:*
> *but whoso shall do and teach them,*
> *the same shall be called great in the kingdom of heaven*
> *(Matt. 5:17-19).*

> Evidently Jesus left no doubt in the mind of his disciples in regard to his loyalty to the commandments and the teachings of the prophets.

ON HIS OWN IDENTITY

Jesus' statements throughout the Bible suggest that any idea of exalting him to divinity was unthinkable. In Matthew's gospel, Jesus denounces in the strongest terms those who exalt him by calling him 'Lord':

> *"None of those who cry out, 'Lord, Lord,'*
> *will enter the kingdom of God*
> *but only the one who does the will of my Father in heaven.*
> *When the day comes, many will plead with me,*
> *'Lord, Lord, have we not prophesied in your name?*
> *Have we not exorcised demons by its power?*
> *Did we not do many miracles in your name as well?'*
> *Then I will declare to them solemnly, 'I never knew you.*
> *Out of my sight, you evil doers!' "*
> **[Matthew 7:21-23]**

Jesus would not even accept the praise of a man who called him good:
> *"Good teacher, what must I do to share in everlasting life?"*
> *Jesus answered: "Why do you call me good?*
> *No one is good but God alone."*
> **[Mark 10:17-18]**

If Jesus would not even allow himself to be called good, he certainly would not claim divine qualities.

Perhaps some of the difficulty that humans have is that we do not really recognize the qualities of God. When we say that He is omnipotent and omniscient, we do not fully realize what that means—that God can do *anything* and that He knows *everything,* including our innermost secrets, and those we are not even aware of yet. Unless we do realize the full meaning of these qualities, it is possible to think of Jesus as having had them. But the next section shows clearly that he did not.

ONLY GOD HAS DIVINE QUALITIES
Matthew 24:36, quoted below, demonstrates that Jesus was not omniscient:
> (In relation to the end of the world Jesus said to them:)
> *"As for the exact day or hour, no one knows it,*
> *neither the angels in heaven nor the son,*
> *but the Father only."*
> **[Matthew 24:36]**

One divine quality is the ability to assign the souls their positions in the Hereafter. Jesus tells us that only God can do this. When he speaks to the mother of his disciples James and John, she asks him to promise that her sons will be on either side of him in the Hereafter:
> *"...But sitting at my right hand or my left is not mine*
> *to give. That is for those to whom it has been reserved*
> *by my Father."*
> **[Matthew 20:23]**

Surely, when Jesus prayed in the Garden of Gethsemane he demonstrated that he was neither omnipotent nor omniscient:

> *"Father, if it is your will,*
> *take this cup from me;*
> *yet not my will but yours be done."*
> **[Luke 22:42]**

Jesus made it clear in many, many ways that he was not God, that God is greater. Nowhere is this more definitely stated than when he spoke to his disciples about his imminent departure:

> *If you truly loved me*
> *you would rejoice to have me go to the Father,*
> *for the Father is greater than I.*
> **[John 14:28]**

JESUS' PRAYER

As demonstrated above, and throughout the Gospels, Jesus prayed to God. This certainly argues against his being God. God would not pray to Himself.

Like Luke 22:42, the Gospel of Matthew reports that a very human Jesus became distressed in Gethsemane and turned to God for solace:

> *He advanced a little and fell prostrate in prayer.*
> *"My Father, if it is possible,*
> *let this cup pass me by.*
> *Still, let it be as you would have it, not as I."*
> **[Matthew 26:39]**

There were times when Jesus felt the need to pray with special urgency. Luke reports that, on one occasion, Jesus prayed very hard:

> *In his anguish, Jesus prayed*
> *with all the greater intensity,*
> *and his sweat became like drops of blood*
> *falling to the ground.*
> **[Luke 22:44]**

Jesus also prayed to God that the people might believe in him as God's messenger. This specifically defines the role of Jesus as deliverer of God's message:

...Jesus looked upward and said,
"Father, I thank you for having heard me.
I know that you always hear me
but I have said this for the sake of the crowd,
that they may believe that you sent me."
[John 11:41-42]

One of the most compelling pieces of evidence that Jesus was not God is in the way that he taught the disciples to pray:

One day he was praying in a certain place.
When he had finished, one of his disciples asked him,
"Lord, teach us to pray, as John taught his disciples."
He said to them, "When you pray, say:
'Our Father in heaven,
hallowed be your name,
your kingdom come,
your will be done
on earth as it is in heaven.
Give us today our daily bread,
and forgive us the wrong we have done
as we forgive those who wrong us.
Subject us not to the trial
but deliver us from the evil one.' "
[Luke 11:1-4]
[Matthew 6:9-13]

Note that Jesus taught us to pray to the Father, our Creator, not to himself. In fact, he did not mention himself in any way, nor did he indicate that we should pray in his name. His instructions were very specific—we are to pray to God alone.

This would not be the case if Jesus himself were God.

REPORTED DYING WORDS

Even in the narration of his death, in the Gospels of Matthew and Mark, there is an incident that contradicts the concept of Jesus' divinity.

According to these two references, Jesus was put on the cross and left to die, then:

> *At that time Jesus cried in a loud voice,*
> *"Eloi, Eloi, Lama Sabachtani?"*
> *which means, "My God, my God,*
> *why have you forsaken me?"*
>
> **[Matthew 27:46] & [Mark 15:34]**

It is not logical that God would ever say: *"My God, my God, why have you forsaken me?"* This utterance was recorded in both Gospels in Jesus' mother tongue, Hebrew/Aramaic, to emphasize the accuracy of transmission. Thus, according to this Christian narration, Jesus could not have been God.

RECENT SCHOLARLY DEVELOPMENTS

There has long been a great deal of debate among Christian theologians and scholars regarding the divinity of Jesus. This debate has intensified in recent years, and there seems to be an increasingly open concern over the truth of this doctrine. For example, the authors of *THE MYTH OF GOD INCARNATE* (The Westminster Press, 1977, p. ix) concluded, as already quoted, that:

> "Jesus was (as he is presented in Acts 2:21) 'a man approved by God' for a special role within the divine purpose, and...the later conception of him as God incarnate, the Second Person of the Holy Trinity living a human life, is a mythological or poetic way of expressing his significance for us."

Other Christian scholars have questioned not only the claims that Jesus is God, but even that he publicly proclaimed himself to be the Messiah. On October 17, 1987, the Associated Press released the following news release:

> ST. PAUL, Minn. (AP) — A group of biblical scholars known as the Jesus Seminar has decided that Jesus did not publicly proclaim himself the messiah.

The scholars say the belief that he did, held by many Christian denominations, was added to biblical texts by early church officials.

The group is meeting at Luther Northwestern Seminary in St. Paul this weekend as part of a five-year effort to reach a consensus on which sayings attributed to Jesus are historically accurate and which were added by others.

Individual scholarly efforts to determine the historical nature of the Gospels, and of Jesus himself, are not new. What is unusual about this group is its effort to reach voting consensus, after study and debate.

The group includes about 125 Roman Catholic, Protestant and non-Christian scholars.

Seminar leaders admit the findings are not to be taken as truth, but rather as a scholarly "theory of uncertainty." One example of the biblical phrases that the group claims are not authentic is in John 11:25, where Jesus said, "I am the resurrection and the life. He who believes in me will...never die."

In concluding that Jesus did not make such messianic claims, the group cites non-canonical and highly controversial sources such as the Gospel of Thomas and the hypothetical "Q document."
(*ARIZONA DAILY STAR*, October 18, 1987)

Significantly, the Jesus Seminar leaders have admitted that their scholarly findings "are not to be taken as truth, but rather as a scholarly *theory of uncertainty.*" In other words, even the leading scholars are still uncertain.

One of the most important outcomes of the 1987 meeting of the Jesus Seminar is the conclusion that the biblical statements in John 11:25-26 are "not authentic." This is relevant to this chapter, since many Christians have stretched the interpretation of these particular verses to mean that Jesus is God:

Jesus told her:
"I am the resurrection and the life:
Whoever believes in me,
though he should die,
will come to life;

*and whoever is alive and believes
in me will never die."*
                    [John 11:25-26]

THE OPPOSING VIEW:
EXAMINATION OF VERSES

We have seen that there is significant scriptural evidence that Jesus was not God. On the other hand, there are numerous other verses understood by many Christians to mean that he was divine. The rest of this chapter examines those verses.

It is appropriate at this time to quote from Michael Goulder, Staff Tutor in Theology, Birmingham University. Goulder states in *THE MYTH OF GOD INCARNATE* (Ibid., p. 48):

> ...In my early ministry I was still a trembling believer in Chalcedonian orthodoxy—Jesus was God the Son, of one substance with the Father, who came down from heaven. Trembling beliefs do not alter themselves: they are reinforced daily by the repetition of the liturgy. When I look back, I think that the firmest plank on which my creed rested was the familiar passage in John 1, "The Word became flesh and dwelt among us...." This was not alone, for there were similar statements in Col. 1 and Phil. 2, and hints of the same in many of the Pauline letters, and in Hebrews. Where had St. John got the doctrine from? Not from Jesus.

In these lines we see some of the Biblical references understood by many people to mean that Jesus is God. We also see in the same lines that Goulder found those roundabout statements do not bestow divinity upon Jesus.

Since Michael Goulder, at least for a period in his life, was a typical Christian, let us look at the biblical references that led him to believe that Jesus was God:

*The Word became flesh
and made his dwelling among us,
and we have seen his glory:
the glory of an only Son*

*coming from the Father
filled with enduring love.*
[John 1:14]

This verse makes a clear distinction between the Word and the Father. In no way does it argue for the divinity of Jesus. The Word comes from God, and thus reflects the glory of the Creator, much as our creations reflect our skills and talents. But the Word cannot logically be considered divine anymore than our handiwork is human.

The first verse of John is more misleading in this regard:

*In the beginning was the Word;
The Word was in God's presence,
and the Word was God.*
[John 1:1]

An objective reading of this verse raises the question: "If the *'Word'* was *'in God's presence,'* how could it be God?" When something is in your presence, it has to be, by definition, separate from you.

The logical understanding is that the 'Word' emanates from God, or **represents God**. When we obey the Word of God, we obey God.

This understanding is confirmed by the fact that throughout the Gospels, Jesus emphasizes that he did not speak on his own, that God told him what to say. This clearly indicates that Jesus delivered the Word of God, not that he was God. Here is an illustration from John:

*Jesus proclaimed aloud: "Whoever puts faith in me
believes not so much in me as in him who sent me;
and whoever looks on me is seeing him who sent me.
I have come into the world as its light, to keep anyone who
believes in me from remaining in the dark.
If anyone hears my words and does not keep them,
I am not the one to condemn him,
for I did not come to condemn the world but to save it.
Whoever rejects me and does not accept my words
already has his judge, namely, the word I have spoken—
it is that which will condemn him on the last day.
For I have not spoken on my own; no, the Father who sent*

*me has commanded me what to say and how to speak.
Since I know that his commandment means eternal life,
whatever I say is spoken just as he instructed me."*
[John 12:44-50]

A distinction is made here among the Word of God, Jesus and God. Perhaps that distinction can be expressed this way: Jesus brought to the world God's Word, and thus, whoever puts faith in that Word, puts faith in God. This distinction is reinforced by the following quotes, again from the Gospel of John:

*I cannot do anything of myself. I judge as I hear,
and my judgment is honest because I am not seeking
my own will but the will of him who sent me.*
[John 5:30]

*"My doctrine is not my own; it comes from him who sent me.
Any man who chooses to do his will
will know about this doctrine—
namely, whether it comes from God
or is simply spoken on my own.
Whoever speaks on his own is bent on self–glorification.
The man who seeks glory for him who sent him is truthful;
there is no dishonesty in his heart."*
[John 7:16-18]

In John 8:40, Jesus describes himself as *"a man who has told you the truth which I have heard from God."* Thus again we see that Jesus delivered the Word of God.

A significant understanding, and one whose relevance cannot be ignored here, occurs in the Quran. The Quran calls Jesus a 'Word' from God. Among Quranic scholars, the prevalent understanding of this description of Jesus is that Jesus was created inside Mary's womb as the result of a 'word' from God, the word 'Be.' Jesus was then formed inside Mary's womb, without the need of a human father:

*The angels said, "O Mary, God sends to you good news:
a **word** from Him to be called the Messiah,
Jesus, the son of Mary.*

*He will be prominent in this world
and, in the Hereafter, he will be among those
close to God."*
[Quran 3:45]

*The creation of Jesus, as far as God is concerned,
is the same as the creation of Adam;
God created him from clay then said to him, "Be,"
and he was.*
[Quran 3:59]

COL. 1—PAUL'S TEACHING

Much of what we recognize today as the basic teachings of Christianity came to us through Paul. Remember that though Paul was the major missionary to the gentiles in the years immediately following the crucifixion, he never met Jesus. All of his understanding of Jesus and what he taught came secondhand and through the visions which he had.

Most of Paul's own teachings come to us through letters which he wrote to various Christian communities. His Epistle to the Colossians is an example. It was partly from this letter that Michael Goulder originally derived the idea of Jesus' divinity:

*He is the image of the invisible God,
the first-born of all creatures.
In him everything in heaven and on earth was created,
things visible and invisible, whether thrones or
dominations, principalities or powers; all were created
through him, and for him.
He is before all else that is.
In him everything continues in being.*
[Col.1:15-17]

This obviously is Paul's teaching, not that of the man who said, *"Why do you call me good? No one is good but God alone"* (Mark 10:18).

In this passage, Paul was using an old Biblical formula to describe Jesus. Wisdom personified was similarly described in Solomon's Proverbs:

> *"The Lord begot me, the firstborn of his ways,*
> *the forerunner of his prodigies of long ago;*
> *From of old I was poured forth, at the first,*
> *before the earth."*
> **[Proverbs 8:22-23]**

> *"Happy the man who obeys me,*
> *and happy those who keep my ways,*
> *happy the man watching daily at my gates,*
> *waiting at my doorposts;*
> *for he who finds me finds life,*
> *and wins favor from the Lord;*
> *but he who misses me harms himself;*
> *all who hate me love death."*
> **[Proverbs 8:33-36]**

When we look carefully at Colossians 1:15–17 and Proverbs 8:22–23 and 8:33–36, we realize that we cannot draw the conclusion that Jesus and Wisdom personified are both God. Rather, both instruct us in the means of reaching God, and thus are God's agents, not God. To paraphrase the authors of THE MYTH OF GOD INCARNATE, these descriptions are a mythological or poetic way of expressing the significance of Jesus and Wisdom for us.

The opening statements of Colossians make a clear distinction between God and Jesus:

> *Paul, an apostle of* **Christ** *Jesus by the will of God,*
> *and Timothy our brother,*
> *to the holy ones at Colossae, faithful brothers in Christ.*
> *May* **God our Father** *give you grace and peace.*
> **[Col. 1:1-2]**

PHILIPPIANS 2

Another biblical statement mentioned by Golder and used by many to convey divinity upon Jesus is in Philippians 2.

This is one of the epistles of uncertain origin. Many scholars do not accept it as being written by Paul at all. A comparison of the King James version and the broader based *NEW AMERICAN BIBLE*, reveals a dramatic difference in the meanings given this statement. Here is the King James version:

Let this mind be in you, which was also in Christ Jesus:
Who, being in the form of God, thought it not robbery
to be equal with God:
But made himself of no reputation,
and took upon him the form of a servant,
and was made in the likeness of men.
[Phil. 2:5-7]

Upon reading these straightforward verses, who can blame a believer in the scripture for believing that God was incarnated into a human being? Here we see that Jesus was *"in the form of God,"* that he *"thought it not robbery **to be equal with God**,"* and that *"he took upon him the form of a servant, and was made in the likeness of men."* No wonder this rendering is frequently quoted with confidence by those who believe in the divinity of Jesus.

However, when we study the original material, a totally different picture emerges. Let us look at the same verses, translated directly from the oldest available texts by the translators of the *NEW AMERICAN BIBLE*, rather than revised from earlier translations, as is the case in the King James version:

Your attitude must be that of Christ:
Though he was in the form of God,
he did not deem equality with God
something to be grasped at.
Rather, he emptied himself and took the form of a slave,
being born in the likeness of men.
He was known to be of human estate.
[Phil. 2:5-7]

Contrary to the King James' assertion that Jesus' equality with God was acceptable to Jesus, the *NEW AMERICAN BIBLE* translation conveys the exact opposite; Jesus deemed it unthinkable. The same problem is observed in the King James translation that Jesus *"made himself of no reputation"* and *"was made in the likeness of men."* This is vastly different from Jesus *"being born in the likeness of men. He was known to be of human estate."*

Ironically, only two verses later, a clear distinction *is* made between God the Supreme Being, and Jesus as one who was exalted by God. Obviously, God would have no need to exalt Himself. Jesus the man was exalted by God. The complete biblical context clearly negates the idea that Jesus was God.

1 TIMOTHY 3:16

Another of the major verses used to support the concept that Jesus is divine is Verse 3:16 of 1 Timothy. However, there is now a developing conviction that this particular verse was an innovation written to conform to the principles of the Nicene Conference. Many scholars question the authenticity of all of 1 Timothy, pointing to strong evidence that Paul wrote only three epistles: Romans, Corinthians and Galatians.

In any case, examination of two different translations of 1 Timothy 3:16 shows how easily the translator's understanding of a verse can overshadow the original wording. The verse in the King James version reads as follows:

And without controversy great is the mystery of godliness:
God was manifest in the flesh, justified in the Spirit,
seen of angels, preached unto the Gentiles,
believed on in the world, received up into glory.
[1 Timothy 3:16]
King James version

Now let us look at this verse in the *NEW AMERICAN BIBLE,* which you will remember is a much more recent translation, able to use a wider range of documents than were available at the time of the King James translation. This translation clearly refers to Jesus, but does not say he is God:

*Wonderful, indeed, is the mystery of our faith,
as we say in professing it:
"He was manifested in the flesh, vindicated in the Spirit;
Seen by the angels; preached among the Gentiles,
Believed in throughout the world, taken up into glory."*
[1 Timothy 3:16]
New American Bible

WORD OF GOD

It seems that the representation of God by His word, as explained earlier, has contributed to occasional confusion. Nevertheless, the idea that the 'Word' of God represents God is common to the three scriptures: the Torah, the New Testament and the Quran:

*I will raise up for them a prophet like you
from among their kinsmen,
and I will put **my words** into his mouth;
he shall tell them all that I command him.
If any man will not listen to
my words which he speaks in my name,
I myself will make him answer for it.*
[Deut. 18:18-19]

This idea that Jesus did not speak on his own is repeated throughout the Gospels, as quoted earlier. See, for example, John 7:16-18 and 12:44-50.

In the Quran, the same principle is set forth:

Whoever obeys the messenger is obeying God.
[Quran 4:80]

Deuteronomy 18:15, and 18-19 (quoted above) indicate that the messenger of God does not speak on his own. Thus, the message delivered by God's messenger and contained in the scripture, stands for the messenger, and represents God (*"If any man will not listen to **my words** which he speaks in my name, I myself will make him answer for it" [Deut. 18:19]*).

In his book, the translated title of which is *THE HISTORY OF RELIGIOUS SECTARIANISM* (The Message Publishers, 1985, p. 23), Dr. Ahmed Mansour, Professor of Islamic History at the famous Azhar University in Cairo, states:

> ...since the messenger, be he Moses, Jesus or Muhammad, is dead, the commandment 'to obey the messenger' must be referring to the message itself.

He also notes that the scriptures consistently order us to "obey the messenger," and not to obey Moses, or Jesus, or Muhammad by name.

This same idea has been expressed by other scholars on the basis of the Quran 11:1-2 and 65:10-11, where the scripture is specifically called *"the messenger."*

> *(This is) a scripture whose verses have been perfectly*
> *designed then elucidated.*
> *It comes from the most wise, the most knowledgeable.*
> *Proclaiming: "You shall not worship except God.*
> *I come to you from Him, as a preacher*
> *and a bearer of good news."*
> **[Quran 11:1-2]**
>
> *...God has sent down to you the scripture,*
> *a messenger reciting for you God's profound revelations....*
> **[Quran 65:10-11]**

JOHN 14

This principle of representing God by His Word is clearly demonstrated in John 14:6-11. It appears that the problem of the deification of Jesus arose from the same kind of misunderstanding of this passage as we witnessed earlier with John 1:1, Colossians 1:15-17 and Philippians 2:5-7.

> *I am the way, and the truth, and the life;*
> *no one comes to the Father but through me.*
> *If you really knew me, you would know my Father also.*
> *'From this point on you know him....*
> *Whoever has seen me has seen the Father.*

How can you say, 'Show us the Father'?
Do you not believe that I am in the Father
and the Father is in me?
The words I speak are not spoken of myself;
it is the Father who lives in me
accomplishing his works.
Believe me that I am in the Father
and the Father is in me,
or else, believe because of the works I do."
[John 14:6-11]

John 14:20 sheds more light on the idea of God being represented by His words, and shows that *"I am in the Father, and the Father is in me"* does not mean that Jesus is the same as God:

"On that day you will know that
I am in my Father, and you in me, and I in you."
[John 14:20]

Obviously, Jesus' disciples do not become Jesus, nor are they made divine when Jesus tells them: *"I am in the Father, and you in me, and I in you."* Similarly, Jesus' statement that *"To hate me is to hate my Father"* (John 15:23) does not mean that Jesus and God are one and the same. Rather it indicates a hatred of the Father's teachings that Jesus delivered.

Thus far it is clear that the references from the New Testament we have examined, which are understood by many to confer divinity upon Jesus, are indirect and misleading. Meanwhile, the direct expression: "Jesus is God" is never found.

ISAIAH 9

Interestingly, it is in the Old Testament where we find the most critical verse for searching Christians—Isaiah 9:6. The translation of this particular verse is the most misleading of all. In the King James version, it reads:

For unto us a child is born, unto us a son is given;
and the government shall be upon his shoulder;

> and his name shall be called
> Wonderful, Counselor, The mighty God,
> The everlasting Father, the Prince of peace.
>
> **[Isaiah 9:6]**
> *King James version*

Let's look at this same verse as translated by the Jewish Publication Society of America in its *THE HOLY SCRIPTURES: According To The Masoretic Text* (Philadelphia, 1917):

> For a child is born unto us, a son is given unto us;
> And the government is upon his shoulder;
> and his name is called
> Pele-joez-el-gibbor-Abi-ad-sar-shalom;
> (That is: Wonderful in council is God the Mighty,
> the Everlasting Father, the Ruler of peace.)
>
> **[Isaiah 9:5]**
> *Torah*

To be named *"Wonderful in council is God the Mighty, the Everlasting Father, the Ruler of peace"* is not to be God, but to be named with a name which glorifies God. The names "John," meaning "God is good," and "Joshua," meaning "God is salvation," are similar.

Note that the original Hebrew is used to ensure and emphasize the accuracy of transmittal. Also note that the verse number is five, rather than the number six of the King James translation.

The verse number five is also retained in the *NEW AMERICAN BIBLE* translation, along with a much more accurate rendition of the Hebrew/Aramaic of the original:

> For a child is born to us, a son is given us;
> upon his shoulder dominion rests.
> They name him wonder-counselor, God-hero,
> Father-Forever, Prince of Peace.
>
> **[Isaiah 9:5]**
> *New American Bible*

Though this translation is not as straightforward as the Jewish rendering of the same verse, the difference between this translation and the King

James version is doctrine-shaking. The difference between the phrases *"the mighty God,"* and *"God-hero"* is obvious and profound. There are people today who can be considered God-heros, doing great work in the cause of God.

REVELATION 1:8
Going back to the New Testament, we see a similar pattern of misunderstanding and mistranslation in another verse often quoted to show that Jesus was God. First, the King James version:

I am Alpha and Omega,
the beginning and the ending, saith the Lord,
Which is, and which was, and which is to come,
the Almighty.

[Revelation 1:8]

Second, *THE NEW AMERICAN BIBLE* version:

The Lord God says,
"I am the Alpha and the Omega,
the One who is and who was
and who is to come, the Almighty!"

[Revelation 1:8]

Note that the King James version omits the critical first line: *"The Lord God says..."* The omission gives the impression that it is Jesus who is speaking, rather than God. This impression is strengthened by the fact that *"I am the Alpha and the Omega"* is repeated some verses later within the context of a mysterious and totally ambiguous story. Here the source of these words is not identified as Jesus, but as *"One like a Son of Man."*

Whether leaving out the crucial first line was intentional or not in the King James version, there is no doubt that its absence creates a false reading of the verse.

JOHN 8:58
There is one last verse we should examine. It also is misunderstood by many who believe that it shows Jesus was divine:

> Jesus answered them: "I solemnly declare it:
> before Abraham came to be, I AM."
> **[John 8:58]**

Extracting divinity for Jesus from this verse is stretching it far beyond its context. First of all, a complete reading of the entire passage leaves a very different impression:

> Jesus answered: "If I glorify myself, that glory comes
> to nothing. He who gives me glory is the Father,
> the very one you claim for your God,
> even though you do not know him. But I know him.
> Were I to say I do not know him,
> I would be no better than you—a liar!
> Yes, I know him well, and I keep his word.
> Your father Abraham rejoiced that he might see my day.
> He saw it and was glad."
> At this the Jews objected: "You are not yet fifty!
> How can you have seen Abraham?"
> Jesus answered them: "I solemnly declare it:
> before Abraham came to be, I AM."
> **[John 8:54-58]**

A very clear distinction is made in this passage between Jesus and God. Also, the idea of Jesus' pre-existence is not at all unique in the Bible and does not prove his divinity. For example, we see the pre-existence of Jeremiah in the Old Testament:

> The word of the Lord came to me thus:
> Before I formed you in the womb I knew you,
> before you were born I dedicated you,
> a prophet to the nations I appointed you.
> **[Jer. 1:4-5]**

Personified Wisdom's pre-existence, in the same manner as Jesus, is reported in Proverbs:

> "The Lord begot me, the firstborn of his ways,
> the forerunner of his prodigies of long ago;
> From of old I was poured forth,

at the first, before the earth.
When there were no depths I was brought forth,
when there were no fountains or springs of water;
Before the mountains were settled into place,
before the hills, I was brought forth;
While as yet the earth and the fields were not made,
nor the first clods of the world."
[Proverbs 8:22-26]

As an interesting note, Jesus, Solomon and Jeremiah are recognized in the Quran as prophets and messengers of God. Furthermore, the Quran states that God made a special covenant with all His messengers before the creation of the heaven and the earth (Quran 3:81).

In fact, according to the Quran, the entire human race predated the heaven and the earth:

Recall that your Lord gathered
all the descendants
of Adam (before creation),
and had them bear witness for themselves,
saying: "Am I not your only Lord?"
They all said, "Yes indeed, we thus bear witness."
[Quran 7:172]

EXAMINATION OF THE TITLE 'LORD'

Finally, we need to look at the title 'Lord' as used to refer to Jesus. This word has sometimes been chosen as the translation instead of 'Master' or 'Rabbi.' In English it has a much more elevated meaning and, when referring to Jesus, it is understood by many readers to imply his divinity. Jesus' own understanding of this title is illustrated in the following verses from Matthew. Note that the Jews were expecting the Messiah (literally 'the anointed one') to come from the family of David:

In turn Jesus put a question to the assembled Pharisees,
"What is your opinion about the Messiah?
Whose son is he?"
"David's," they answered.

> *He said to them, "Then how is it that David*
> *under the Spirit's influence calls him 'lord,' as he does:*
> *'The Lord said to my lord,*
> *Sit at my right hand,*
> *until I humble your enemies*
> *beneath your feet'?"*
>
> **[Matthew 22:41-44]**
> *New American Bible*

Here we see a clear distinction between the Lord God who supports His Messiah, humbling his enemies and keeping him in His protection (at His right hand), and that same Messiah as a 'lord' or master/rabbi.

The irony of the above scriptural quote has been masked by the translation rendered as 'lord', which might also be translated as 'father'. The latter translation then becomes:

> *..."Whose son is he?"*
> *"David's," they answered.*
> *He said to them, "Then how is it that David...calls him 'father,'*
> *as he does: 'The Father said to my father....' "*
>
> **[Matthew 22:42-44]**
> *Modified New American Bible*

In the Middle East, the traditional title for the father, the head of the household or the leader is *'rabb'* or 'lord.' This is true in Hebrew, Aramaic and Arabic. It does not necessarily imply divinity.

CONCLUSION

Jesus followed the Mosaic law and did not claim divinity. According to the Bible, He was not omniscient nor omnipotent.

We have examined a large number of scriptural references which are often used to support the divinity of Jesus. As we have seen, there are factors in all of them which negate that conclusion, or make it very questionable. Given the fact that nowhere in the Bible do we see a direct identification of Jesus as God, and that Jesus strongly upheld all the commandments and emphasized the First Commandment, we can only conclude that the doctrine of Jesus' divinity has no foundation in the scripture nor in the life and teachings of Jesus. This concept is an innovation in Christian doctrine.

This may be a painful and radical conclusion for many. Painful because it is new and runs contrary to what we have always been taught. Radical only if we are not familiar with the historical development of the doctrine of Christ's divinity.

Chapter Four

WHERE DID THE CONCEPT COME FROM?

...The source of your unity and election is genuine suffering which you undergo by the will of the Father and of Jesus Christ, our God. Hence you deserve to be considered happy....you are imitators of God; and it was God's blood that stirred you up once more to do the sort of thing you do naturally and have now done to perfection.
—Ignatius, Bishop of Antioch

Within a hundred years, the concept of Jesus as God was already well established. Bishop Ignatius was the second bishop of Antioch. He was killed around 100 A.D. The above excerpt is from his letter to the Ephesians (*EARLY CHRISTIAN FATHERS*, C. C. Richardson, ed., Macmillan, 1970, pp. 87-88).

It is important to examine how and why the concept of Jesus as God developed and became accepted. That understanding helps us to assess our own beliefs. For that reason, this chapter will give you some historical and theological perspective on the development of this idea of Jesus as God incarnate.

The concept developed very early, but it was not universally accepted among the vanguard of Christianity. There was great diversity among early Christians.

EARLY DIVERSITY

Even in the newborn church, immediately after Jesus' death, there were major differences among the Jewish Christians and the Gentile Christians. These are indicated in the New Testament book of Acts. During his journeys, Paul went to Jerusalem, where he met with James and the elders of the early church. In the next verses they are addressing him:

> *"You see brother, how many thousands of Jews have
> come to believe, all of them staunch defenders of the law.
> Yet they have been informed that you teach the Jews
> who live among the Gentiles to abandon Moses,
> to give up the circumcision of their children,
> and to renounce their customs.
> What are we to do about your coming, of which
> they are sure to hear? Please do as we tell you.
> There are four men among us who made a vow.
> Take them along with you and join with them
> in their rite of purification;
> pay the fee for the shaving of their heads. In that way,
> everyone will know that there is nothing in what they have
> been told about you, and that you follow the law yourself
> with due observance.
> As for the Gentile converts, we sent them a letter with our
> decision that they were merely to avoid meat
> sacrificed to idols, blood, the flesh of strangled animals,
> and illicit sexual union."
> Accordingly, Paul gathered the men together and went
> through the rite of purification with them the next day.
> Then he entered the temple precincts to give notice of
> the day when the period of purification would be over,
> at which time the offering was to be made for each of them.*
> **[Acts 21:20-26]**

This passage shows that the early Jewish Christians continued to follow Jewish law, circumcising their sons and keeping the traditions of their fathers. Some of them even continued to take the Nazarite vow, as the four men whose heads were being shaved. This Mosaic practice was one of dedicating oneself to God and following strict rules of purity and sacrifice for a specified length of time. (See Numbers 6:1-21.)

Gentile converts, on the other hand, often did not follow the same set of rules. It is apparent from the above verses that in the Jerusalem church they had only to abstain from forbidden meats and adultery.

Besides differing practices, there were also many different understandings within the early church concerning the true identity of Jesus. In fact, these differences were very marked, and are eloquently expressed by Robert L. Wilken in *THE MYTH OF CHRISTIAN BEGINNINGS* (Doubleday, 1971, pp. 165-166):

> There were no set beliefs agreed on by all; nor were there any ground rules on how to determine what to say or think or do; nor was there any acknowledged authority for deciding such question (sic). Let us suppose that in the year A.D. 35 two men, Michael and Ephraim, became Christians in Jerusalem; Michael went to the town of Edessa in Syria to live, and Ephraim went to Alexandria in Egypt. On arrival in their respective cities, each told others about the remarkable man Jesus. After telling their friends about Jesus, let us say Michael and Ephraim organized Christian congregations. Almost immediately, problems would arise. What should we do about the Jewish law? What should we do when we gather for worship?... The questions were endless, and the Christians in Edessa and the Christians in Alexandria would not answer all in the same way—the traditions Michael and Ephraim brought with them were too embryonic, too undefined, to answer every new question or settle every dispute. They had to make up their own minds as they understood their own situation and the memories they brought with them.
>
> Now let us change the scene to A.D. 75. Forty years have passed. In the meantime the Jews have been defeated by the Romans, and Jerusalem has been destroyed. Also, the Christian movement has spread widely and solidified its traditions. Let us now suppose that someone from Edessa travels to Alexandria and learns that there is a Christian community there.... To his surprise, he learns that they have little in common except a common loyalty to Jesus, and the fragments of his words that have been handed on orally. And even the fragments

of his sayings are not in quite the form they are in Edessa. The visitor from Edessa discovers that the Christians in Alexandria do not keep the Jewish law, whereas his congregation keeps it exactly, admitting no one to the Christian community without circumcision. The Alexandrians pray to Jesus, whereas in Edessa all prayers are addressed solely to God the Father.... Both are shocked at the practices and beliefs of the others.

Given this great diversity among early Christians, at what point did the doctrine of Jesus' divinity actually develop? And what were the factors contributing to the spread and eventual formalization of this doctrine?

Searching for the answers to these questions is especially difficult because there are no known surviving documents from the 'Mother Church', the original Christian community in Jerusalem. For an extensive discussion of this point, see S.G.F. Brandon's book *JESUS AND THE ZEALOTS* (Charles Scribner's Sons, 1967, pp. 148–159). We will review his arguments in a few pages.

But first, we need to look more closely at the differences that Paul had with other followers of Christ. Remember that Paul never met Jesus, nor did he study with the original apostles. His knowledge of Jesus and his teachings came mostly through personal inspiration. Hyam Maccoby states (*THE MYTHMAKER*. Harper and Row, 1987, pp. 3-4):

> Paul claimed that his interpretations were not just his own invention, but had come to him by personal inspiration; he claimed that he had personal acquaintance with the resurrected Jesus, even though he had never met him during his lifetime. Such acquaintance, he claimed, gained through visions and transports, was actually superior to acquaintance with Jesus during his lifetime, when Jesus was much more reticent about his purposes.

Clearly Paul, however good his motivations, could not pass on to us the exact words or actions of Jesus during the years he taught on earth. He had no way of knowing exactly what they were.

It is inevitable that he would be in some conflict with those who were actually with Jesus during those years. Their experiences and their memories of a flesh and blood man would necessarily be different from the Jesus he knew from his visions.

PAUL vs THE SUPER-APOSTLES

There are many indications in Paul's letters that there were powerful and authoritative opponents to his teachings. Paul wrote that these opponents were teaching a *"gospel other than the gospel you accepted"* and preaching about *"another Jesus:"*

> *My fear is that, just as the serpent seduced Eve*
> *by his cunning, your thoughts may be corrupted and*
> *you may fall away from your sincere*
> *and complete devotion to Christ.*
> *I say this because when someone comes preaching another*
> *Jesus than the one we preached, or when you receive*
> *a different spirit than the one you have received,*
> *or a gospel other than the gospel you accepted,*
> *you seem to endure it quite well.*
> *I consider myself inferior to the "super-apostles" in nothing.*
> **[2 Corinthians 11:3-5]**

As Paul continues, it is clear that those whom he refers to above as the *'super-apostles'* are Hebrews whose authority he does not question, but he tries to match their qualifications with his own: *"Since many are bragging about their human distinctions, I too will boast"* (2 Cor. 11:18).

Brandon argues that Paul's *'super-apostles'* are indeed the original Apostles of Jesus (Ibid., pp. 152-153):

> Paul, curiously, despite his exceeding agitation over their activity, never names them. Whoever they were, they were obviously Christians of great authority or representative of leaders of great authority; for they were able to go among Paul's own converts and successfully present a rival interpretation of the faith. Moreover, although he is so profoundly disturbed by their action, Paul never questions their authority as they did his. These facts, taken together with Paul's very evident embarrassment about his relations with the leading Apostles at Jerusalem, point irresistibly to one conclusion only: that the 'other gospel', which opposes Paul's own, was the interpretation of the nature and mission of Jesus propounded by the Jerusalem Church, which comprised the original Apostles of Jesus and eyewitnesses of his life.

Not all Biblical scholars agree that the *'super apostles'* were the original apostles, and that the *'other gospel'* was that of the Jerusalem Church, but there is a very good case for their being so. In fact, the very name *'super apostles'* is evidence. Who else would fit such a name?

The passage we quoted earlier from Acts 21:20-26 demonstrates that the original apostles had differing views from Paul, and they had the authority to enforce those views, at least by writing to the Gentile converts to *"avoid meat sacrificed to idols, blood, the flesh of strangled animals, and illicit sexual union."*

This is important because since Paul never met Jesus, he had no first hand knowledge of Christ's teachings. Yet most of what we know about the very early years of Christianity comes from Paul's letters. And the Gospel of Christ which has survived has come through the Pauline tradition. All of this means that we do not know for certain what the original followers of Jesus taught. And more importantly, we do not know how much of Christ's own teaching has reached us unflavored by Paul's understanding.

One thing we do know is that the differences among the early members of the church were deep and divisive. Paul's letter to the Galatians makes that clear. Scathingly, Paul exhorts his readers to stick to the gospel he had delivered to them:

"I am amazed that you are so soon deserting him who called you in accord with his gracious design in Christ, and are going over to another gospel....
For if even we, or an angel from heaven, should preach to you a gospel not in accord with the one we delivered to you, let a curse be upon him!"
[Galatians 1:6-8]

Obviously, whoever Paul's opponents were, they had authority that Paul felt he needed to counteract. This is shown by the fact that he goes on by defending his own authority, and then attacking those who apparently were preaching a return to Mosaic law:

> *"All who depend on observance of the law,*
> *on the other hand, are under a curse."*
> **[Galatians 3:10]**

In fact, the above verse shows that Paul actively fought against those who observed Mosaic law. This is reinforced by the following verses:

> *"I point out once more to all who receive circumcision*
> *that they are bound to the law in its entirety.*
> *Any of you who seek your justification in the law*
> *have severed yourselves from Christ and fallen from God's favor!"*
> **[Galatians 5:3-4]**

One of the strongest pieces of evidence that Paul's opponents were the original apostles comes in Galatians 2:6-14:

> *Those who were regarded as important,*
> *however (and it makes no difference to me how prominent*
> *they were—God plays no favorites), made me add nothing.*
> *On the contrary, recognizing that I had been entrusted*
> *with the gospel for the uncircumcised...those who were*
> *the acknowledged pillars, James, Cephas, and John,*
> *gave Barnabas and me the handclasp of fellowship,*
> *signifying that we should go to the Gentiles*
> *as they to the Jews.... When Cephas came to Antioch*
> *I directly withstood him, because he was clearly*
> *in the wrong. He had been taking his meals with*
> *the Gentiles before others came who were from James.*
> *But when they arrived he drew back to avoid trouble with*
> *those who were circumcised. The rest of the Jews*
> *joined in his dissembling, till even Barnabas was swept*
> *away by their pretense. As soon as I observed that*
> *they were not being straightforward about the truth*
> *of the gospel, I had this to say to Cephas in the presence*
> *of all: "If you who are a Jew are living according*
> *to Gentile ways rather than Jewish, by what logic do you*
> *force the Gentiles to adopt Jewish ways?"*
> **[Galatians 2:6-14]**

We see here that initially it was James, Cephas and John who recognized Paul's authority. What about the other Jerusalem apostles? Were they the important and prominent ones who wanted Paul to add to his teachings? If not, why were they not mentioned? And what was he supposed to add? It is logical that these opponents were original apostles, and that they wanted him to preach the following of Mosaic law.

Later, in Antioch, even Cephas had a run-in with Paul over the practice of Mosaic law. Paul accuses him and the other Jews of dissembling, and not being straightforward about the truth of the gospel and of wanting to force the Gentiles to accept Mosaic law. If Paul attacked even his supporters among the Jerusalem apostles, it is inevitable that he was at odds with them as a group.

Given the extremely strong prohibition of idol worship in any form, which is at the base of Mosaic law, it is almost certain that any tendency to deify Jesus would have been strongly resisted by the Jerusalem apostles. This could well have been the basic cause of the rift between Paul and the original apostles.

Brandon argues (Ibid., p. 154):

> According to Paul's own testimony, his 'gospel' was repudiated and his authority as apostle was rejected by his opponents. This the leaders of the Jerusalem Church could effectively do, because Paul had never been an original disciple of Jesus, nor had he learned the faith from them. However, the irony of the situation, from our point of view, is that it is Paul's 'gospel' that has survived and is known to us from his own writings, whereas the 'gospel' of the Jerusalem Christians can only be reconstructed from what may be inferred from Paul's references to it and what may be culled, also by inference from the Gospels and Acts. This apparent triumph of Paul's version of the faith is surely to be traced to the Jewish overthrow in A.D. 70....

That final sentence is of great importance. Brandon draws a parallel between the esoteric Jewish community at Qumran whose books were hidden before the community was destroyed by the Romans in A.D. 68. Those documents are now known as the Dead Sea Scrolls, and the community which authored them is known almost solely through them.

Recently those very scrolls have been made available to scholars at large, stirring great hopes for break throughs in our understanding of Judaism at the time of Christ and thus, early Christian development.

Brandon proposes that the Christian community in Jerusalem, which strongly maintained its ties to Judaism, was also wiped out by the Romans in A.D. 70, and its documents lost, as a repercussion of the Jewish uprising there.

The annihilation of the Mother Church of Jerusalem meant that the original leaders of Jewish-Christianity were killed or dispersed. Also, there must have been a strong political force encouraging the moving away from Judaism and any traditions which identified a community as being tied to Judaism. These factors would have greatly aided in the strengthening and spread of non-Jewish concepts among early Christians. They would have especially helped the spread of the concept of Jesus' deification.

THE MYTH OF GOD INCARNATE: THEOLOGICAL EXAMINATION

Let us diverge now from the historical aspects of this discussion and examine some of the theological aspects. The whole doctrine of Jesus' divinity has been thoroughly examined in *THE MYTH OF GOD INCARNATE* (Ed. J. Hick, Westminister Press, 1977). This important books is not readily available now. Therefore, I have quoted extensively from it.

One look at the list of Christian scholars who contributed to this collection shows that it is not a radical fringe among today's theologians who reject this doctrine of incarnation, rather it is a growing number of careful and highly qualified theologians:

Don Cupitt: University Lecturer in Divinity and Dean of Emmanuel College, Cambridge (UK).
Michael Goulder: Staff Tutor in Theology in the Department of Extramural Studies at Birmingham University.

*John Hick: H. G. Wood Professor of Theology at
    Birmingham University.
Leslie Houlden: Principal of Ripon College, Cuddesdon.
Dennis Nineham: Warden of Keble College, Oxford.
Maurice Wiles: Regius Professor of Divinity and Canon of
    Christ Church of England's Doctrine Commission.
Frances Young: Lecturer in New Testament Studies at
    Birmingham University.*

From the Preface of THE MYTH OF GOD INCARNATE (Ibid., p. ix):

> The writers of this book are convinced that another major theological development is called for in this last part of the twentieth century. The need arises from growing knowledge of Christian origins, and involves a recognition that Jesus was (as he is presented in Acts 2.21) 'a man approved by God' for a special role within the divine purpose, and that the later conception of him as God incarnate, the Second Person of the Holy Trinity living a human life, is a mythological or poetic way of expressing his significance for us. This recognition is called for in the interests of truth....For Christianity can only remain honestly believable by being continuously open to the truth.

In the same book (Ibid., p. 4), Maurice Wiles writes:

> Negative generalizations are notoriously dangerous claims to make. Nevertheless, it seems to me that throughout the long history of attempts to present a reasoned account of Christ as both fully human and fully divine, the church has never succeeded in offering a consistent or convincing picture.

Mr. Wiles, who is canon of Christ Church, goes on to urge that "Christianity without incarnation" should be regarded as a positive and constructive idea, rather than negative and destructive. He points out that the worship of Christ, "traditional throughout the whole of Christian history," is "idolatrous in character."

Some three centuries after Jesus' death, culminating with the Nicene Conferences of 325 A.D., a politically motivated church solidified the doctrine of 'God Incarnate.'

In *THE MYTH OF GOD INCARNATE* (Ibid., p. 17), Francis Young makes an interesting and critical observation, pointing out that the focus of the Gospels is quite different from that of Jesus' own teachings:

> The epistles of Paul – and indeed the speeches of Acts – reveal that the early Christian gospel was about Jesus Christ. This makes it the more likely that the gospels correctly report that the message of Jesus was different – it was about the kingdom of God.... There are difficulties in tracing explicit Messianic claims back to Jesus himself. Apart from John where interpretative material is clearly placed upon the lips of Jesus, the gospels invariably portray not Jesus but others as using phrases like the 'Holy One of God', or 'Son of David', or 'Son of God'.... Furthermore, Mark's gospel conveys the impression that Jesus attempted to keep his identity as Messiah a secret divulged only to his inner circle. This 'Messianic secret' motif in Mark remains an unsolved problem, especially since it appears sometimes to be introduced rather artificially; yet it adds to the impression that Jesus may well have preferred to remain enigmatic, in the interests of directing his hearers away from false enthusiasm for himself, to the consequences of the coming of God's kingdom for their lives here and now.

Young goes farther, arguing that Paul never claimed Jesus was God (Ibid., p. 20-22). Whether Paul himself believed Jesus to be God, or not, it was the Pauline tradition which eventually developed the doctrine of God incarnate, culminating with its formal doctrinal statement in the Nicene Creed.

In *THE MYTH OF GOD INCARNATE* Michael Goulder and Frances Young present a number of plausible theories dealing with the development of incarnational belief in the early church. They both agree that the roots of incarnation and of the divinity of men extend to the pre-Christian and pagan cultures.

We know that the concept of 'son of God' was quite different for Jews following Mosaic law and Romans whose religious mythology specifically referred to divine children of the gods. Young points out that both Jewish and Greco-Roman traditions have the idea of the ascent of exceptional men into heaven, and of heavenly beings—either angels or gods—coming to earth to help men. It is not an impossible step from those traditions to the belief that God Himself had to come to earth to save mankind.

Don Cupitt, Dean of Emmanuel College at Cambridge concluded that the incarnational doctrine no longer belongs to the essence of Christianity, "but only to a certain period of church history, now ended" (Ibid., p. 134).

Cupitt also narrates that the Eastern theologian John of Damascus (about A.D. 675-749), in defending iconolatry, admitted the fact that neither the Trinity nor the *homoousion* [identifying Jesus as God] nor the two natures of Christ can be found in the scriptures. John of Damascus then continued, "but we know those doctrines are true."

After he acknowledged that icons, the Trinity and the incarnation are innovations, John of Damascus went on to urge his readers to hold fast to them "as venerable traditions delivered to us by the fathers." Thus, at least 14 centuries ago, he recognized that the incarnation doctrine is not a divinely revealed doctrine, delivered to us by Jesus, but a human idea passed down to us "by the fathers."

Don Cupitt adds that John of Damascus was not the only theologian to use this argument. Theodore the Studite (about A.D. 795-826) adopted it too. Cupitt then states that this "brings out an odd feature of Christianity, its mutability and the speed with which innovations [such as the incarnational doctrine] come to be vested with religious solemnity to such an extent that anyone who questions them finds himself regarded as the dangerous innovator and heretic."

Cupitt emphasizes that the idea of God incarnate in the person of Jesus Christ is in direct contradiction with the teachings of Jesus. He points out (Ibid., p. 138):

> ...The Bible contains (Ex. 20.4) a categorical prohibition, not merely of any kind of image of God, but of any naturalistic or representational art, a prohibition which has influenced Jews and Muslims to this day. Nothing other than God can be an adequate image of God, and God himself, being transcendent, cannot be delineated. Early Christianity

inherited and followed this rule. Old Testament arguments against idolatry, pagan arguments and early Christian arguments ran closely parallel.

The distortion the doctrine of God incarnate causes is well stated in Cupitt's conclusion (Ibid., p. 140):

> The assertion that deity itself and humanity are permanently united in the one person of the incarnate Lord suggests an ultimate synthesis, a conjunction and continuity between things divine and things of this world.... This idea distorts Jesus' ironical perception of disjunction between the things of God and the things of men, a disjunction particularly enforced in the parables.... Whether he is seen as an apocalyptic prophet or as a witty rabbi (or, as I think, both), what matters in Jesus' message is his sense of the abrupt juxtaposition of two opposed orders of things.... But the doctrine of the incarnation unified things which Jesus had kept in ironic contrast with each other, and so weakened the ability to appreciate his way of speaking, and the distinctive values he stood for.

John Hick, H. G. Wood Professor of Theology at Birmingham University, compares the exaltation of Jesus to the status of God with the deification of Buddha in Buddhism. He blames the innovation of the incarnation doctrine on a human tendency to elevate the founder of any given religion. He states (Ibid., p.170):

> Buddhology and christology developed in comparable ways. The human Gautama came to be thought of as the incarnation of a transcendent, pre-existent Buddha as the human Jesus came to be thought of as the incarnation of the pre-existent Logos or divine Son. And in the Mahayana the transcendent Buddha is one with the Absolute as in Christianity the eternal Son is one with God the Father.... We are seeing at work a tendency of the religious mind which is also to be seen within the history of Christianity. The exaltation of the founder has of course taken characteristically different forms in the two religions. But in each case it led the developing traditions to speak of him in terms which he himself did not use, and to understand him by means of a complex of beliefs which was only gradually formed by later generations of his followers.

Where Did the Concept Come From? 63

Each essay in THE MYTH OF GOD INCARNATE is a careful piece of honest scholarship and soul searching commentary. Such work requires the moral courage to step out of one's upbringing, indeed, out of one's culture, and allow the objective examination of one's own faith. The unanimous conclusion of these courageous theologians is that the concept of God incarnate is indeed innovation and not part of the teachings of Jesus Christ.

The results of this innovation are clearly and eloquently summarized by Don Cupitt (Ibid,. pp. 142, 143, 145):

> If in Jesus the fullness of God himself is permanently incarnate, Jesus can be directly worshipped as God without risk of error or blasphemy. A cult of Christ as distinct from a cult of God then becomes defensible, and did in fact develop. The practice of praying direct to Christ in the Liturgy, as distinct from praying to God through Christ...slowly spread, against a good deal of opposition, eventually to produce Christocentric piety and theology. An example of the consequent paganization of Christianity was the agreement to constitute the World Council of Churches upon the doctrinal basis of 'acknowledgement of our Lord Jesus Christ as God and Saviour'—and nothing else. Perhaps it was only when Christocentric religion finally toppled over into the absurdity of 'Christian Atheism' that some Christians began to realize that Feuerbach might have been right after all; a Chalcedonian christology could be a remote ancestor of modern unbelief, by beginning the process of shifting the focus of devotion from God to man.... Similarly, it could not resist the giving of the title *Theotokos*, Mother of God, to Mary. The phrase 'Mother of God' is *prima facie* blasphemous, but it has had a very long run, and the orthodox have actively promoted its use, fatally attracted by its very provocativeness.

> ....It is my contention that the doctrine of Christ as God's divine son has here humanized deity to an intolerable degree. The strangeness of it is seldom noticed even to this day. A sensitive theologian like Austin Farrer can dwell eloquently upon a medieval icon of the Trinity, and a philosopher as gifted as Wittgensten can discuss Michelangelo's painting of God in the Sistine Chapel, and in neither case is it noticed that there could be people to whom such pagan anthropomorphism is abhorrent, because it signifies a 'decline of religion' in the only sense that really matters, namely, a serious corruption of faith in God.

CONCLUSION

We have seen that there was great diversity in the beliefs of early Christians. The understanding that Jesus was God comes to us from one line of those early believers, those who followed Paul. Paul himself never met Jesus, and his views differed radically from the original apostles who did know Jesus and followed his example directly. The destruction of the original Christian community in Jerusalem allowed Paul's understanding to overshadow that of the original followers of Jesus.

From a theological point of view we have seen that there were many possible factors contributing to the development of the doctrine of God incarnate. The influence of pagan belief undoubtedly played a part, as did the natural human tendency to exalt the founder of any religion. We also see that there are highly qualified Christian scholars who reject the concept outright, and offer very convincing arguments for doing so.

Chapter Five

WAS HE THE SON?

All who are led by the Spirit of God are sons of God.
[Romans 8:14]

Jesus was the son. But whose son? He has been called the Son of Man, the Son of God, the Son of Mary, and the Son of David. Whose son was he? And what does that mean for us?

SON OF MAN
Throughout the Gospels, Jesus almost always calls himself the 'Son of Man.' It is the most frequently used title for him. In all cases but one it is used by Jesus to describe himself. Since he was born of a virgin, without any contribution from a man, this name which he used for himself, stresses his human nature. It stresses the fact that he was of human descent, not a descendant of God. If this were not true, the term 'Son of Woman' would have been much more appropriate.

Vincent Taylor points out that in Jewish scripture and tradition the term 'son of man' was used as a synonym for 'man' (*THE NAMES OF JESUS*, St. Martin's Press, 1953, pp. 325, 330). The Psalms illustrate this:

What is man, that you should be mindful of him,
or the son of man
that you should care for him?
[Psalm 8:5]

May your help be with the man of your right hand,
with the son of man whom you yourself made strong.
[Psalm 80:18]

But what about all the references Jesus makes to God as his 'Father'? Do they not indicate that he was God's son? Yes, but not in the way most Christians understand. Remember, since God gave us life, we are all His children in that sense. This fact is clearly stated in the Old Testament.

OLD TESTAMENT REFERENCES
TO GOD'S 'FATHERHOOD'
About five centuries before Jesus was born, the writer of the Old Testament book of Malachi spoke of God's 'Fatherhood' to mankind:

Have we not all the one Father?
Has not the one God created us?
Why then do we break faith with each other,
violating the covenant of our fathers?
[Malachi 2:10]

Jesus' reference to God as his father was part of the idiom of his day, as it had been for those who came before him. An earlier Jesus wrote the Old Testament book of Sirach. The book of Sirach is not accepted by Protestants, but the Catholic Church has always accepted it as an inspired part of the canon. This earlier Jesus, son of Eleazar, also addressed God as 'Father':

Who will set a guard over my mouth,
and upon my lips an effective seal,
That I may not fail through them,
that my tongue may not destroy me?
Lord, Father and Master of my life, permit me not to fall by them!
[Sirach 22:27-23:1]

I called out: O Lord, you are my father,
you are my champion and my savior....
[Sirach 51:10]

This practice of calling God 'Father' is also shown by the way that Jesus taught his disciples to pray:
> *Our Father who art in heaven,*
> *Hallowed be thy name...*
> **[Matthew 6:9]**
> **[Luke 11:2]**

JESUS NOT THE ONLY ONE CALLED 'SON'
This allegorical expression is used often in the Bible. Many are called sons of God—individuals as well as groups of people, like the Children of Israel:
> *"So you shall say to the Pharaoh:*
> *Thus says the Lord: Israel is my son, my first born.*
> *Hence I tell you: Let my son go, that he may serve me.*
> *If you refuse to let him go, I warn you,*
> *I will kill your son, your first-born."*
> **[Exodus 4:22-23]**

These verses demonstrate for us what being God's son means. Obviously God was not saying that the Children of Israel were literally his first born son. Rather, the phrase indicates that God loved the nation of Israel as if they were a first born son.

The Psalms refer to the expected Messiah as the son of God. They also call the angels the sons of God:
> *"He shall say of me,*
> *'You are my father, my God, the rock, my savior.'*
> *And I will make him the first-born,*
> *highest of the kings of the earth."*
> **[Psalm 89:27-28]**

> *For who in the skies can rank with the Lord?*
> *Who is like the Lord among the sons of God?*
> **[Psalm 89:7]**

So far we have seen verses which refer to the Children of Israel, the expected Messiah and the angels as God's sons. This in itself makes it clear that sonship in the Bible has a different meaning from what we normally understand.

All of the examples we have looked at so far come from the Old Testament. What about in the New Testament? In the New Testament, Adam is called God's son.

Luke's genealogy of Jesus ends with Adam, whom Luke says is the *"son of God:"*

> *When Jesus began his work he was about thirty years of age,*
> *being—so it was supposed—the son of Joseph, son of Heli,*
> *son of Matthat, son of Levi, son of Melchi*
> *...son of Enos, son of Seth, son of Adam, son of God.*
>
> **[Luke 3:23-38]**

Clearly, if Adam was the son of God, then Jesus could not have been His only son.

Luke was Paul's companion, so it is not surprising that Paul also makes the point that Jesus was not God's only son:

> *All who are led by the Spirit of God are sons of God.*
> *You did not receive a spirit of slavery leading you back into fear,*
> *but a spirit of adoption through which we cry out,*
> *"Abba!" (that is, "Father").*
> *The Spirit himself gives witness with our spirit*
> *that we are children of God.*
> *But if we are children, we are heirs as well:*
> *heirs with Christ, if only we suffer with him so as to be*
> *glorified with him.*
> *I consider the sufferings of the present to be as nothing*
> *compared with the glory to be revealed in us.*
> *Indeed, the whole created world eagerly awaits*
> *the revelation of the sons of God.*
> *Creation was made subject to futility,*
> *not of its own accord but by him who*
> *once subjected it; yet not without hope,*

*because the world itself will be freed
from its slavery to corruption
and share in the glorious freedom
of the children of God.*
[Romans 8:14-21]

Jesus was not the only son of God. The phrase itself means something other than what we understand in ordinary usage. What does it mean?

MEANING OF SONSHIP

Jesus and his followers obviously had a very different concept of what the title 'Son of God' meant from the understanding which the Greeks had. In *THE NAMES OF JESUS* (Ibid, p. 54), Taylor gives us a good idea of what those opposing concepts were:

> The significance of the phrase in Jewish thought is reasonably clear; it does not describe a divine being, but characterizes groups of individuals who stand in a particularly close religious relationship with God...
>
> Strange to Jewish thought, with its strong emphasis on monotheism, the idea of 'divine men'...or 'sons of god'...was congenial to the Greek mind. It is therefore possible to argue that, while primitive Christianity confessed Jesus as 'the son of God' the content of the idea was determined by Hellenistic usage.

Here Taylor, himself a Christian, gives us some very important information. It was the influence of Greek and Roman thought which distorted the original scriptural meaning of sonship to God. The Old Testament makes it clear that all of God's true adherents are sons of God. Those who love God, and whom He loves in return, are His children. For example, we see that in the Book of Job the angels are referred to as the sons of God:

> *One day, when the sons of God came to present themselves
> before the Lord, Satan also came among them.*
> **[Job 1:6]**

*Where were you when I founded the earth?
Tell me, if you have understanding.*

Who determined its size; do you know?
Who stretched out the measuring line for it?
Into what were its pedestals sunk, and who laid the cornerstone,
While the morning stars sang in chorus and
all the sons of God shouted for joy?
[Job 38:4-7]

We have already seen that in Exodus the nation of Israel is called God's son. This idea is repeated in the Book of Hosea where the children of Israel are called *"children of God":*

The number of the Israelites shall be like the sand of the sea,
which can be neither measured nor counted.
Whereas they were called, "Lo-ammi (not my people),"
They shall be called, "Children of the living God."
[Hosea 2:1]

In the New Testament, Jesus often indicated that the righteous are children of God. The Lord's prayer shows this. So does the fact that Jesus referred to God as *"my father and your father":*

Jesus then said, "Do not cling to me,
for I have not yet ascended to the Father.
Rather, go to my brothers and tell them, 'I am ascending
to my father and your father, to my God and your God.' "
[John 20:17]

Those who followed Jesus are called *"sons of God"* in the King James version and *"children of God"* in THE NEW AMERICAN BIBLE:

Any who did accept him he empowered to become children of God.
These are they who believe in his name—
who were begotten not by blood,
nor by carnal desire, nor by man's willing it, but by God.
[John 1:12-13]

In fact, Jesus taught that there is only one father for us all, God:

> *"Do not call anyone on earth your father.*
> *Only one is your father, the One in heaven."*
> **[Matthew 23:9]**

This again indicates that we should devote ourselves wholeheartedly to God alone—with "all our hearts, all our minds, all our souls and all our strength." No human relationship can stand in the way of that devotion.

We learn from Jesus' teachings that God is called *'Father,'* because He is the Creator, the Sustainer and the Provider for all of us:

> *It is not for you to be in search of what*
> *you are to eat or drink. Stop worrying.*
> *The unbelievers of this world are always running after these things.*
> *Your Father knows that you need such things.*
> *Seek out instead his kingship over you,*
> *and the rest will follow in turn.*
> *Do not live in fear, little flock.*
> *It has pleased your Father to give you the kingdom.*
> **[Luke 12:29-32]**

If you devote yourself to God, He will make all things work for your good, as only a divine Father can:

> *We know that God makes all things work together*
> *for the good of those who love him,*
> *who have been called according to his decree.*
> *Those whom he foreknew*
> *he predestined to share the image of his son*
> *that the son might be the first-born of many brothers.*
> **[Romans 8:28-29]**

CHILDREN BY CHOICE

Paul's epistle to the Philippians clearly shows that we are children of God as a result of our free choice. We choose to be children of God by doing His will:

> *In everything you do, act without grumbling or arguing;*
> *prove yourselves innocent and straightforward,*
> *children of God beyond reproach*

*in the midst of a twisted and depraved generation—
among whom you shine like the stars of the sky.*
[Philippians 2:14-15]

Jesus taught that we become children of God by being born spiritually. Such spiritual birth, or being *"begotten from above,"* is attained by keeping God's commandments. Such spiritual birth is attainable by anyone:

*A certain Pharisee named Nicodemus,
a member of the Jewish Sanhedrin, came to him at night.
"Rabbi," he said, "we know you are a teacher come from God,
for no man can perform signs and wonders such as you
perform unless God is with him."
Jesus gave him this answer: "I solemnly assure you, no one
can see the reign of God unless he is begotten from above."
"How can a man be born again once he is old?"
retorted Nicodemus. "Can he return to his mother's womb
and be born over again?"
Jesus replied, "I solemnly assure you,
no one can enter into God's kingdom
without being begotten of water and Spirit.
Flesh begets flesh, Spirit begets spirit.
Do not be surprised that I tell you
you must all be begotten from above."*
[John 3:1-7]

VERSES INDICATING EXCLUSIVE SONSHIP

What about those Biblical references to Jesus as the 'only' son of God, or even 'the only begotten son'?

The most prominent verse concerning Jesus' sonship to God, and the most frequently quoted, is John 3:16:

*Yes, God so loved the world that he gave his only Son,
that whoever believes in him
may not die but may have eternal life.*
[John 3:16]

Was He the Son? 73

There are only three other verses, significantly also in the Gospel of John, that refer to Jesus as the only son. They are John 1:14 and 18, and John 3:18:

*The Word became flesh and made his dwelling among us,
and we have seen his glory:
the glory of an only Son coming from the Father,
filled with enduring love.*
[John 1:14]

*No one has ever seen God. It is the only Son,
ever at the Father's side, who has revealed him.*
[John 1:18]

*Whoever believes in him avoids condemnation,
but whoever does not believe is already condemned
for not believing in the name of God's only Son.*
[John 3:18]

It is extremely important to realize that the Gospels of Matthew, Mark and Luke **never** state that Jesus was God's only son. This is even more significant when we realize that the Gospel of John was the last Gospel written.

According to the translators of *THE NEW AMERICAN BIBLE*, the Gospels of Matthew and Mark were written shortly after the year 70 A.D., and the Gospel of Luke is dated to "approximately 75 A.D." The Gospel of John was the last, written between 90 and 100 A.D., at a time when we know the doctrine of Jesus' divinity was already well established. This fact is demonstrated by Bishop Ignatius' quote at the beginning of Chapter Four.

GOSPEL OF JOHN
In Chapter Two we discussed who actually wrote the Gospel of John. Because of its importance in the present discussion, let me recap: In their *Introduction to the Books of the New Testament* the translators of *THE NEW AMERICAN BIBLE* present the almost universally ac-

cepted theory that the Gospel of John was written by someone other than John, probably a disciple, and then edited later by another disciple (Ibid., p. xxxvii).

References to inconsistencies within the Gospel of John are made by the same translators:

> However, more and more students of this gospel are coming to believe that ... inconsistencies were probably produced by subsequent editing in which homogeneous materials were added to a shorter original. Other difficulties for the theory of eyewitness authorship are presented by the gospel's highly developed theology, and by certain elements of its literary style. For instance, some of the miracles of Jesus have been worked into highly dramatic scenes (ch 9); there has been a careful attempt to have the miracles followed by discourses which explain them (chs 5 and 6); the sayings of Jesus have been woven into long discourses of a quasi-poetic form resembling the speeches of personified Wisdom in the Old Testament.
> (*THE NEW AMERICAN BIBLE*, p. xxxvii)

In other words, the Gospel of John was written not so much to present the historical facts about the life of Jesus Christ, but to present and explain already established dogma. Translators also note special problems in translating the Gospel of John:

> The Gospel according to John comprises a special case. Absolute fidelity to his technique of reiterated phrasing would result in an assault on the English ear that would be almost unendurable. Yet the softening of the vocal effect by substitution of other words and phrases would destroy the effectiveness of his poetry. Again, resort is had to compromise.
> (*THE NEW AMERICAN BIBLE*, p. xxxvii)

In John 1:14 and 18 and John 3:16 and 18, the word 'only' directly contradicts the numerous assertions that all righteous people are sons of God, and the Biblical references to others, like Israel, as God's first-born son.

Paul himself did not believe Jesus to be God's begotten son. In Romans he explains that Jesus was *"descended from David according to the flesh"* and then *"made son of God in power according to the spirit of holiness..."* (Romans 1:3-4). The *NEW AMERICAN BIBLE* has a footnote saying that the later phrase could also be translated as *"was declared"* or *"was proclaimed the powerful son of God."*

Whether Jesus was made, declared or proclaimed the son, this is clearly a different kind of sonship, one we can all strive for.

Only two verses before the description of Jesus as God's only son in John 3:16, the gospel's author calls Jesus Son of Man.

In fact this whole section of verses needs to be examined together:
> *Just as Moses lifted up the serpent in the desert,*
> *so must the Son of Man be lifted up,*
> *that all who believe may have eternal life in him.*
> *Yes, God so loved the world that he gave his only Son,*
> *that whoever believes in him*
> *may not die but may have eternal life.*
> *God did not send the Son into the world to condemn the world,*
> *but that the world might be saved through him.*
> *Whoever believes in him avoids condemnation,*
> *but whoever does not believe is already condemned*
> *for not believing in the name of God's only Son.*
> **[John 3:14-18]**

If these are the actual words of Jesus, as the translators would have us believe, why would he not say *"that the world might be saved through me"* and *"Whoever believes in me avoids condemnation"*?

The second of the three verses which refer to Jesus as the only son, John 1:18, also shows the human tendency to lean toward distortions which fit our preconceived understanding. The rendition shown of this verse is essentially the King James version because in the *NEW AMERICAN BIBLE* they translate it: *"...It is God the only Son, ever at the Father's side, who has revealed him."* However, the footnote for this verse reads:

> Many commentators regard these verses as explanation rather than part of the pre-Prologue hymn. *God the only Son:* other MSS read "the Son, the only one" or "the only Son".

Given the fact that other manuscripts do not indicate that Jesus is God, the *NEW AMERICAN BIBLE* translation of this verse is clearly incorrect. This error makes the whole verse suspect, and indeed we see in the footnote that many scholars do not accept it as part of the pre–Prologue hymn. It may well have been a note in the margin which got incorporated into the text in the process of copying, as discussed in Chapter Two.

QURANIC VIEW

A large segment of the monotheistic world considers the idea of Jesus' exclusive 'begotten' sonship of God to be a gross blasphemy. After reflecting on the greatness of God as revealed recently by scientific facts, and discussed in a later chapter, one can understand this point of view. The Quran, for example, states that *"the mountains are about to crumble"* at the thought that the great and Almighty God has begotten a son:

> *They said, "God most gracious has begotten a son!"*
> *You have committed a gross blasphemy.*
> *The heavens are about to explode from such a blasphemy,*
> *the earth is about to tear asunder,*
> *and the mountains are about to crumble,*
> *because they claim that the Most High has begotten a son.*
> *Everyone in the heavens and the earth,*
> *before the Most High, is no more than a servant.*
> *He has numbered each and every one of them.*
> *Each and every one of them will come before Him on the*
> *Day of Resurrection as a single (helpless) individual.*
> *As for those who believe and lead a righteous life*
> *the Most High will shower them with love.*
> **[Quran 19:88-96]**

CONCLUSION

As God shows us in Matthew 23:9, John 20:17 and Romans 8:14, those who use their free will to abide by God's commandments continue to enjoy the privilege of sonship to God, while those who disregard the commandments are children of the devil.

Was He the Son?

Only the most recent gospel, the Gospel of John, written after sufficient time for religious innovations to begin to form, states that Jesus was God's only son.

Note also that the alteration of the biblical concept of "Son of God" into the idea of a divine son, and then into the trinitarian doctrine "God the Son" is consistent with the human tendency to idolize that which is most important to us. This tendency may be very natural, but it hampers us from totally devoting ourselves to God the Father, and thus becoming children of God ourselves.

> *The heavens proclaim your wonders,*
> *O Lord, and your faithfulness,*
> *in the assembly of the holy ones.*
> *For who in the skies can rank with the Lord?*
> *Who is like the Lord among the sons of God?*
> **[Psalm 89:6-7]**

Chapter Six

THE TRINITY: FACT OR FICTION?

> 1. A Christian is one that believes things his reason cannot comprehend... 2. He believes three to be one, and one to be three; a Father not to be elder than his Son; a Son to be equal with his Father; and one preceding from both to be equal with both; he believing three persons in one nature, and two natures in one person. 3. He believes a virgin to be a mother of a son, and that very son of hers to be her Maker. He believes Him to have been shut up in a narrow room whom heaven and earth could not contain. He believes Him to have been born in time who was and is from everlasting. He believes Him to have been a weak child, carried in arms, who is the Almighty; and Him once to have died who only hath life and immortality in himself.
>
> — Francis Bacon
> (WORKS, vol vii, p.410)

Lord Francis Bacon, the seventeenth century philosopher and Chancellor of England who wrote these words, was obviously a believer in the Trinity. The essay quoted consists of thirty-four such "Christian Paradoxes" which illustrate his belief that: "The more absurd and incredible any divine mystery is, the greater honor we do to God in believing it...." (as quoted by James Yates, *A VINDICATION OF UNITARIANISM*, Wells & Lilly, 1816, p. 278).

The Trinity has always been a mystery. In fact, it is usually described as a divine mystery. When I was young I asked several good Christians to explain the Trinity to me. I was told that the Trinity must be accepted on faith because we cannot always understand the ways of God. Such an answer requires the acceptance that blind faith is a virtue.

The concept of Trinity is that "the Father is God, the Son is God, and the Holy Spirit is God, and yet there are not three Gods but one God" (as stated in one of the critical statements of the doctrine, the Athanasian Creed). These three are all thought of as uncreated, eternal and omnipotent.

You can see why a confused student is told to accept on faith alone!

All this seems to have been confusing for early Christians too. Before the controversy over the Trinity came to a head in the Councils of Nicene during the fourth century, there were many different understandings of the nature of Christ, and an even wider range of understandings about the Holy Spirit. There were those who believed that Jesus was just a mortal man who had a very special relationship with God. Then there were those who agreed with Theodotus of Byzantium that Jesus was born a mere man and attained the ability to work miracles at the time of his baptism. Some of Theodotus' students later believed that Jesus became God after his resurrection. And then there were those known as Monarchians who believed that God and Jesus were one and the same from the beginning of time.

Many of those same views are still held today by various groups of Christians.

SCRIPTURAL EVIDENCE

What do we know about the early belief in the Trinity? Clearly the strong Jewish tradition among the first Christians slowed the initial development of the doctrine. This is especially true since Jesus never preached it. The only place in the gospels that even hints at the doctrine of the Trinity are the last verses of Matthew:

Jesus came forward and addressed them in these words:
"Full authority has been given to me both in heaven and on earth;
go, therefore, and make disciples of all the nations.
Baptize them in the name 'of the Father, and of the Son,
and of the Holy Spirit.' "
        [Matthew 28:18-19]

Nor is the doctrine stated in the Epistles or the Acts of the Apostles. In fact, there is no place in the Testaments, Old or New, which speaks directly of the Trinity.

The whole concept also runs contrary to many verses and themes in the Bible. The most obvious of these is monotheism itself. The next few verses demonstrate this point clearly.

Jesus made it clear that there is only one God:
> *Eternal life is this: to know you, the only true God....*
> **[John 17:3]**

God is 'Almighty.' God uses this word only as a description of Himself:
> *When Abram was ninety-nine years old,*
> *the Lord appeared to him and said:*
> *"I am God the Almighty...."*
> **[Genesis 17:1]**

'Almighty' means by definition that He has *all* power. There is nothing and no one else with any real power. All power stems from God, and it is not shared by anyone.

No one else can ever fit that word! There is only One who is Almighty:
> *I am God, there is no other;*
> *I am God, there is none like me.*
> **[Isaiah 46:9]**

HISTORICAL DEVELOPMENT

The recognition of the Trinity as an innovation started very early in Christian history. Back in the seventh century, the Eastern theologian John of Damascus, in defending his icons, stated that icons were as unscriptural as the Trinity: "You will not find in scripture the Trinity or the homoousion [of the same essence as God] or the two natures of Christ either."

Yet, having acknowledged that icons, the Trinity and the incarnation are innovations, John of Damascus continued to defend them because they were "venerable traditions delivered to us by the fathers." (See *THE MYTH OF GOD INCARNATE*, p. 133.)

The trinitarian doctrine developed gradually over several centuries, through numerous controversies. There were many influences in its formulation and development: the Apostles Creed (around A. D. 160), the Arian controversy (about A. D. 318 to 380), the Nicene Council (A. D. 325), the Council of Constantinople (A. D. 381), the Council of Chalcedon (A. D. 451), and the Athanasian Creed (about A. D. 460) are the major ones.

The Council of Nicaea in 325 initiated the Trinity formula in its statement that the Son is "of the same essence [*homoousios*] as the Father," even though it said very little about the Holy Spirit. Over the next half-century, Athanasius defended and refined the Nicene formula. By the end of the fifth century, the doctrine of the Trinity had taken essentially the form it has today.

The Nicene Creed was originally written in Greek. Its principal liturgical use is in the Eucharist in the West and in both Baptism and the Eucharist in the East. The following text has the additions used only by the Western Church in brackets:

> I believe in one God the Father Almighty; maker of heaven and earth, and of all things visible and invisible. And in one Lord Jesus Christ, the only begotten Son of God, begotten of the Father before all worlds [God of God], Light of Light, very God of very God, begotten, not made, being of one substance [essence] with the Father; by whom all things were made; who, for us men and for our salvation, came down from heaven, and was incarnate by the Holy Ghost of the Virgin Mary, and was made man; and was crucified also for us under Pontius Pilate; he suffered and was buried; and the third day he rose again, with glory, to judge both the quick and the dead; whose kingdom shall have no end.
>
> And [I believe] in the Holy Ghost, the Lord and Giver of Life; who proceedeth from the Father [and the Son]; who with the Father and the Son together is worshipped and glorified; who spake by the Prophets.
>
> And [I believe] in one Holy Catholic and Apostolic Church. I acknowledge one Baptism for the remission of sins; and I look for the resurrection of the dead, and the life of the world to come. Amen.

The historical development of the Nicene Creed is more complex than most people realize. It was long assumed that the creed was initially stated in the council of 325 and then enlarged in 381 at the Council of Constantinople. Discovery of documents from the period has changed that assumption. What we now take to be the Nicene Creed may actually have been based on a pre-existing baptismal creed which was enlarged and first stated at the Council of Constantinople.

We know from the proceedings of the Robber Council that there was more than one version of the Nicene Creed in existence at the time of its convening in 449. This council was called to judge the case of the elderly head of a local monastery whose understanding of the nature of Christ was in question. This monk cited an earlier text of the creed than was currently in use, causing quite a bit of excitement and debate in the council (see Robert L. Wilken, *THE MYTH OF CHRISTIAN BEGINNINGS,* Doubleday & Co., 1971).

Even before the formalization of the Nicene Creed, the persecution of those with non–trinitarian views began. For example, the bishop of Antioch was condemned in a synod held there around 270 for his reported belief that Jesus was a human being in whom the Word of God dwelt, much as a person's reason dwells in him. This was just the forerunner of centuries of similar persecution against those who did not conform exactly to the accepted doctrine of the time.

So far what we have mentioned concerns the controversy surrounding the various understandings of the nature of Christ. There was an equally vehement dispute around the *Filioque* clause which is: *"and the Holy Spirit...who proceedeth from the Father and from the son."* This addition of the son's participation in the Holy Spirit's existence was gradually introduced starting in the 6th century. It is accepted only in the Western Church. The Eastern Church still rejects it as a theological error. Thus the controversy continues.

THEOLOGICAL ASPECTS

We have touched on the historical aspects of the development of this doctrine, but what of the psychological and theological aspects?

John Hick, H. G. Wood Professor of Theology at Birmingham University, and editor of *THE MYTH OF GOD INCARNATE*, attributes the development of the Trinity doctrine to a human tendency to exalt the religion's founder beyond his true identity. As mentioned in Chapter Two, he finds a parallel in the Buddhist trinitarian doctrine which was never preached by Buddha. Hick sums up the doctrine of the Trinity as follows:

> Returning, then to the theme of the exaltation of a human being to divine status, the understanding of Jesus which eventually became orthodox Christian dogma sees him as God the Son incarnate, the Second Person of the Trinity living a human life. As such he was, in the words of the 'Nicene' creed, 'the only-begotten Son of God, Begotten of the Father before all ages, Light of Light, true God of true God, begotten not made, of one substance with the Father'. But this is...far from anything that the historical Jesus can reasonably be supposed to have thought or taught....

The expression "God the Son," an important component of the Trinity, is never found in the gospels. John Hick points out that "as Christian theology grew through the centuries it made the very significant transition from 'Son of God' to 'God the Son,' the Second Person of the Trinity" (Ibid., p. 175).

The Trinity as an innovation is illustrated well by Michael Goulder, Staff Tutor in Theology at Birmingham University:

> ...I went to visit a patient in hospital. I had to wait, and was shortly joined by two further Christian ministers, the one a Congregationalist, the other (in my opinion at the time) of an even lower breed, completely without the law. There being nothing else to do, we fell naturally to theological disputation, and in the course of time the sister was somewhat startled to come in as my Congregationalist friend was saying, 'Well, one thing is certain; he didn't think he was the Second Person of the Trinity'. I found the remark doubly annoying — partly because I had always supposed that Jesus thought he was the Second Person of the Trinity (although wisely not mentioning the fact), and now it was said, it somehow had the ring of the obvious. And partly also I did not relish being enlightened by a minister not of the established church. (Ibid, p. 48)

When we look at the Nicene Creed we easily see the human tendency to exaggerate and to exalt the founder of a religion beyond his own wishes. Referring to Jesus as "God of God" and "very God of very God" clearly reveals excessive emotionalism and exaggeration. One is reminded of the folk wisdom that: "Anything that exceeds the limits, turns to the opposite." When love exceeds the limits it becomes unbearable jealousy and possessiveness; it turns into hate. Obviously, the writers of the Nicene Creed aimed at endearing and exalting Jesus in the eyes of their followers. Their zealous attempts led to serious distortions of Jesus' message—to a point that would be horrifying to Jesus himself:

"None of those who cry out 'Lord, Lord,'
will enter the kingdom of God
*but **only** the one who does the will of my Father in heaven.*
When that day comes, many will plead with me,
'Lord, Lord, have we not prophesied in your name?
Have we not exorcised demons by its power?
Did we not do many miracles in your name as well?'
Then I will declare to them solemnly,
'I never knew you.
Out of my sight, you evildoers!' "
[Matthew 7:21-23]

We cannot study the subject of the Trinity without looking at the views of other, more recent scriptures. The Quran, for example, condemns in the strongest possible terms both the concept of Jesus' divinity and the Trinity:

Unbelievers indeed are those who
say that the Messiah, Son of Mary, is God.
The Messiah himself said, "O Children of Israel,
you shall worship only God,
my Lord, and your Lord."
Certainly, anyone who sets up an idol to rank with God,
God has forbidden for him Paradise;
his sure destiny is the hellfire.
Such evildoers will have no helpers.

*Unbelievers indeed are those
who say that God is one third of a trinity.
Absolutely, there is no other god besides the One God.
Unless they abstain from such utterances
such unbelievers will incur painful retribution.
Would they not repent before God and seek His forgiveness?
God is forgiver, merciful.
The Messiah, son of Mary, was no more than a messenger
like the messengers who preceded him, and his mother was a saint.
Both of them used to eat the food.
Note how we clarify the revelations for them,
then note how they still deviate.
Proclaim: "Would you idolize, besides God,
those who possess no power to harm you or benefit you?"
God is the only One who is the hearer, the omniscient.*
             [Quran 5:72-76]

CONTINUING UNITARIAN vs TRINITARIAN DEBATE

It is important to realize that the debate between Unitarians and Trinitarians continues today, and that a significant segment of modern Christians do not accept the Trinity as a valid doctrine. One denomination even calls themselves the Unitarians.

A typical modern-day unitarian Christian view of the Trinity was published in recent years by a group named "Unity" (Unity Village, Missouri 64065). In their book entitled *THE MAGNIFICENT TOOLS OF THE MIND*, Eric Butterworth writes:

> The term "Holy Spirit" is an important but greatly misunderstood word in Christianity. It is thought of as one part of the Trinity (God in three persons); thus, it is clothed with a kind of individuality which comes and goes in our experience. The concept of the Trinity did not originate with Jesus. It is not even vaguely suggested in his teachings. It was a term that came into being as a result of an effort by the bishops of the early church to define the indefinable. It was a teaching symbol that may have had meaning in its time and among the people of that

day. However, it needs to be clearly redefined in terms of contemporary insights and integrated into the "new model of the universe."

SUMMARY

The doctrine of the Trinity does not originate in the gospels, or in the teachings of Jesus. It demonstrates the human tendency to exalt the object of our love and admiration.

The Nicene creed is the most commonly known statement of the doctrine, but many events shaped its development. The doctrine was formulated over the third and fourth centuries, amid much discussion and controversy.

It still produces much discussion and controversy.

Chapter Seven

SACRIFICIAL LAMB OF GOD?

One of the basic doctrines of modern Christianity is that Jesus was crucified, suffered greatly, and died a humiliating death in order to redeem mankind from its sins. The corollary to this doctrine is that one must accept Jesus as a personal savior to enter the kingdom of God.

For many Christians these concepts have had the unfortunate effect of making Jesus the one to pray to, rather than to God. If you believe that someone will save you it is natural that you will implore him.

For other sincere believers this whole issue has led to doubt. In some cases, this doubt has given rise to theories which question the validity of the crucifixion. Such theories range from the unusual to the bizarre. Usually the theory is that someone else was crucified in Jesus' place or that he survived the event and went on to live and preach in one or more geographical locations.

REASONS FOR DOUBT
Perhaps one of the reasons that these doubts and theories exist is that, from a purely logical point of view, the Christian concept of the crucifixion is in conflict with God's qualities of omnipotence and mercy. The combined doctrines of Jesus' sonship to God and of his crucifixion create a picture of a helpless deity who cannot defend his offspring, or worse yet, a heartless one who deliberately created the circumstances under which his child was required to suffer greatly.

There is another crucial issue here—the issue of individual responsibility. The idea of a single individual atoning for the sins of humanity is in conflict with the concepts of free will and personal responsibility. One of the basic principles of western democracy is that no man can be held accountable for the mistakes of another. Each person is individually responsible for his own actions, with the freedom to make his own decisions and to reap the gain or loss resulting from those decisions.

This concept certainly is not foreign to the scriptures. The theme that "you reap what you sow" threads throughout the Bible:

When God, in the beginning, created man,
he made him subject to his own free choice.
If you choose you can keep the commandments;
it is loyalty to do his will.
There are set before you fire and water;
to whichever you choose, stretch forth your hand.
[Sirach 15:14-16]

The Old Testament book of Sirach has always been accepted by the Catholic Church as canonical and divinely inspired, but it will not be familiar to Protestant readers, who will not find it in their Bibles. The above quote demonstrates the Biblical principle of freedom of choice. The next quote demonstrates that we are punished or rewarded according to those free choices which we make.

Great as his mercy is his punishment;
he judges men, each according to his deeds.
A criminal does not escape with his plunder;
a just man's hope God does not leave unfulfilled.
Whoever does good has his reward,
which each receives according to his deeds.
[Sirach 16:12-14]

It is in the New Testament that we actually find the phrase *"A man will reap only what he sows"*:

Each man should look to his conduct;
if he has reason to boast of anything,
it will be because the achievement is his and not another's.

> *Everyone should bear his own responsibility....*
> *A man will reap only what he sows.*
> **[Galatians 6:4-7]**

The Quran also strongly supports this doctrine of individual responsibility:

> *Say, "You are not responsible for our crimes,*
> *nor are we responsible for what you do."*
> **[Quran 34:25]**

It clearly states that no one can take on the sins of another. Each of us is individually accountable to God:

> *No soul bears the sins of another soul.*
> *Every human being is responsible for his own works.*
> **[Quran 53:38-39]**

GOD AS SAVIOR

The issue of Jesus Christ as savior comes into the picture here. If each man reaps what he sows, how can Jesus be the savior? How could he have taken on the sins of mankind, or negated them? Only the One who can accept repentance and wipe out sins can do that.

Indeed, throughout the Old Testament, God alone is referred to as the savior:

> *David sang the words of this song to the Lord*
> *when the Lord had rescued him*
> *from the grasp of all his enemies and from the hand of Saul.*
> *This is what he sang:*
> *"O Lord, my rock, my fortress, my deliverer,*
> *My shield, the horn of my salvation,*
> *my stronghold, my refuge, my savior,*
> *from violence you keep me safe."*
> **[2 Samuel 22:1-3]**

In Isaiah God Himself speaks, saying clearly that He alone is the savior:

> *For I am the Lord, your God,*
> *the Holy One of Israel, your savior....*

It is I, I the Lord;
there is no savior but me.
[Isaiah 43:3 & 11]

He repeats this categorical statement in Hosea:
I am the Lord, your God, since the land of Egypt;
You know no God besides me,
and there is no savior but me.
[Hosea 13:4]

CONCEPT OF JESUS AS SAVIOR

It is only in the New Testament that Jesus is mentioned as the savior of men. Even then, the Gospels use the term only twice to refer to Jesus. This is noted by Vincent Taylor (Ibid., p. 107-108):

> The name 'the Saviour' was not used by Jesus Himself, and traces of its presence in the Gospel tradition are few and of late date. The only Synoptic example is Lk. ii. 11, in the angelic message to the shepherd, where Jesus is described as 'a Saviour, which is Christ the Lord' ....More surprising is the presence of only a single example in the Fourth Gospel, in Jn. iv 42, where the Samaritans say of Jesus, 'This is indeed the Saviour of the world'.

Besides the two occurrences referred to by Taylor, the only other occurrence in the Gospels clearly refers to God, not Jesus:

Then Mary said:
"My being proclaims the greatness of the Lord,
my spirit finds joy in God my savior,
For he has looked upon his servant in her lowliness...."
[Luke 1:46-48]

There is a related concept, the idea of 'Redeemer.' In *Strong's Exhaustive Concordance of the Bible,* all of the references for this word are from the Old Testament (most in Isaiah) and all refer to God alone. Here are just two as examples:

Thus says the Lord, your redeemer,
who formed you from the womb:

*I am the Lord, who made all things,
who alone stretched out the heavens;
when I spread out the earth, who was with me?*
[Isaiah 44:24]

*You shall know that I, the Lord am your savior,
your redeemer, the mighty one of Jacob.*
[Isaiah 60:16]

God is the Savior and Redeemer of mankind. The concept that Jesus had to suffer a painful and humiliating death in order to save mankind is not in accordance with the scripture, nor does it make sense. Why would a merciful and omnipotent God require such a thing?

WHY IS THERE SUFFERING?

The inevitable question arises: If Jesus was God's son in the sense that "all the righteous are sons of God," why does God allow suffering to afflict anyone? If God cares about His creation, why doesn't He abolish all suffering and render the world perfectly happy and secure?

Many of the remaining chapters of this book deal with these critical questions. But right now we just need to know that there is very strong evidence that Jesus, in fact, did not suffer at all. This startling statement is explained in detail along with scriptural evidence in Chapter Thirteen. In summary, Jesus' body was tortured and crucified *after* the real person of Jesus, i.e., his soul, had departed. Jesus had completed his mission, and his soul had departed at a precisely predetermined moment *prior to any torture or crucifixion.* Jesus' tormentors were unknowingly torturing and crucifying an empty shell devoid of any feeling. Jesus did not suffer at all.

GOD'S CHILDREN DO NOT SUFFER

God's children do not suffer. This appears to be an unrealistic concept, but it is prevalent throughout the scripture. In the Old Testament, we read the following:

*You who dwell in the shelter of the Most High,
who abide in the shadow of the Almighty,
Say to the Lord, "My refuge and my fortress,
my God, in whom I trust."
For he will rescue you from the snare of the fowler,
from the destroying pestilence.
With his pinions he will cover you,
and under his wings you shall take refuge;
his faithfulness is a buckler and a shield.
You shall not fear the terror of the night
nor the arrow that flies by day;
Not the pestilence that roams in darkness
nor the devastating plague at noon.
Though a thousand fall at your side,
ten thousand at your right side, near you it shall not come.
Rather with your eyes shall you behold
and see the requital of the wicked,
Because you have the Lord for your refuge;
you have made the Most High your stronghold.
No evil shall befall you, nor shall affliction come near your tent,
For to his angels he has given command about you,
that they guard you in all your ways.
Upon their hands they shall bear you up,
lest you dash your foot against a stone.
You shall tread upon the asp and the viper;
you shall trample down the lion and the dragon.*
[Psalm 91:1-13]

This Psalm proclaims a consistent biblical premise: that God's children are fully protected from suffering. This is in direct contradiction with any doctrine requiring the kind of suffering that Jesus—one of God's favorite children—supposedly endured. The Psalmist informs us that God *"has given command to his angels that they guard you in all your ways. Upon their hands they shall bear you up, lest you dash your foot against a stone."*

Yes, there are exceptions to this biblical rule, but such exceptions can be explained. The righteous must first pass what can be termed "admission tests," before being admitted into God's kingdom. Once the candidate is proven to be unshakably devoted to God, he or she is admitted into God's grace and perfect happiness.

The example of Job is a perfect illustration. We are told that Satan challenged Job's piety, and was allowed to afflict Job, within limits imposed by God, in order to prove Job's sincerity and steadfastness in his devotion to God:

But Satan answered the Lord and said,
"Is it for nothing that Job is God-fearing?
Have you not surrounded him and his family
and all that he has with your protection?
You have blessed the work of his hands,
and his livestock are spread over the land.
But now put forth your hand and touch anything that he has,
and surely he will blaspheme you to your face."
And the Lord said to Satan,
"Behold, all that he has is in your power;
only do not lay a hand upon his person."
So Satan went forth from the presence of the Lord.
[Job 1:9-12]

Satan proceeded to test Job with affliction after affliction, but Job was not shaken from his devotion:

Job ...cast himself prostrate upon the ground,
and said, "Naked I came forth from my mother's womb,
and naked shall I go back again.
The Lord gave and the Lord has taken away;
blessed be the name of the Lord!"
In all this Job did not sin, nor did he say anything
disrespectful of God.
[Job 1:20-22]

When Job had proven himself and passed all of Satan's tests, God removed the afflictions:

*Also, the Lord restored the prosperity of Job,
after he had prayed for his friends;
the Lord even gave to Job twice as much as he had before.*
[Job 42:10]

Once the tests were over, Job was accepted as a "child of God" and was generously rewarded for his steadfastness in the face of the suffering inflicted upon him by Satan.

The New Testament confirms the idea of perfect happiness for God's children. A good example is found in Luke 12:28-31 where God's children are exhorted to *"stop worrying"* about the provisions of this world. They are told that God is fully aware of their needs, and will automatically fill such needs once they belong with Him:

*If God clothes in such splendor the grass of the field,
which grows today and is thrown on the fire tomorrow,
how much more will he provide for you, O weak in faith!
It is not for you to be in search of what you are to eat or drink.
Stop worrying. The unbelievers of this world are always
running after these things.
Your father knows that you need such things.
Seek out instead his kingship over you,
and the rest will follow in turn.*
[Luke 12:28-31]

CONCLUSION

The scripture clearly tells us that we each "reap what we sow." Jesus will not save us. God, not Jesus, is the savior of each and every one of us. He is the one we must pray to. He is the one we must be devoted to.

Furthermore, God guarantees protection for those who become His children by their devotion. Once admitted into God's protection, there is no real suffering for God's children.

As the story of Job shows us, Satan is the inflictor of suffering. This suffering is inflicted, within strictly imposed limits, upon those undergoing the "admission tests" prior to entering God's protection, or upon those who freely choose to remove themselves from God's domain.

In accordance with these biblical guidelines, Jesus never suffered during the last days of his life.

These guidelines apply to all of God's children:
*All who are led by the Spirit of God
are sons of God.*
[Romans 8:14]

Chapter Eight

WHO IS GOD?

*When I behold your heavens,
the work of your fingers.
The moon and stars which you set in place—
What is man that you should be mindful of him,
or the son of man that you should care for him?*
[Psalm 8:4-5]

Next to God, man is totally insignificant. The Supreme Being is the creator, sustainer and ruler of the universe. This is the basic belief common to all monotheistic religions.

Who is this One common deity? Who is God?

The scriptures tell us that God is the omniscient, omnipotent, omnipresent deity who controls all affairs and every atom in the universe. There is no room for any partners, human or otherwise. Realizing this clarifies why we must follow Jesus' teaching to devote ourselves completely to God.

PHILOSOPHICAL AND THEOLOGICAL DOUBTS
While our knowledge has increased through the ages, many of our best minds have turned away from religion because of the obvious contradictions given out as 'religious truth.' As a result, there is a general lack of knowledge concerning the true identity of God.

Even among religious and theological authorities, doubts abound concerning the description and characteristics of God. There seems to be a consensus that it is impossible to prove or disprove the existence of God, let alone His omnipotence and omniscience. The contemporary philosopher, Mortimer Adler, expressed this. In his book *HOW TO THINK ABOUT GOD* (Macmillan Publishing Co., New York, 1980, p. 16), Adler states:

> In the three monotheistic religions of the West — Judaism, Christianity, and Islam — the proposition that God exists is not an article of faith or religious belief. The first article of faith in all three religions is that God has revealed himself to us in Holy Writ or Sacred Scripture. This, of course, entails the affirmation that the God who has revealed himself exists.

Recently, some recognized religious leaders, both Jewish and Christian, have questioned God's omnipotence. Rabbi Harold S. Kushner wrote in his bestseller of the early eighties, *WHEN BAD THINGS HAPPEN TO GOOD PEOPLE* (Avon Books, New York, 1981, Page 45):

> If we have grown up, as Job and his friends did, believing in an all-wise, all-powerful, all-knowing God, it will be hard for us, as it was hard for them, to change our way of thinking about Him (as it was hard for us, when we were children, to realize that our parents were not all-powerful, that a broken toy had to be thrown out because they could not fix it, not because they did not want to). But if we can bring ourselves to acknowledge that there are some things God does not control, many good things become possible.
>
> We will be able to turn to God for things He can do to help us, instead of holding on to unrealistic expectations of Him which will never come about. The Bible, after all, repeatedly speaks of God as the special protector of the poor, the widow, and the orphan, without raising the question of how it happened that they became poor, widowed, or orphaned in the first place.

Kushner's point of view is made even clearer later in his book. In his chapter entitled: *"God Can't Do Everything, But He Can Do Some Important Things."* On page 148, he asks:

> Are you capable of forgiving and loving God even when you have found out that He is not perfect, even when He has let you down and

disappointed you by permitting bad luck and sickness and cruelty in His world, and permitting some of those things to happen to you? Can you learn to love and forgive Him despite His limitations...?

These words coming from a prominent Jewish religious figure are unexpected. Equally unexpected is that at its publication a prominent Christian—Norman Vincent Peale—called Kushner's book: "A book all humanity needs."

Between the philosophers who have resigned themselves to the notion that God's existence cannot be proven or disproven, and the religious leaders who deny God's omnipotence, it is clear that despite the knowledge explosion that has catapulted us into the space age, most of us are still in the dark ages as far as God is concerned.

SEARCH FOR PROOF

A few years ago, Mortimer Adler drew a distinction between 'faith' in God and 'knowing' that God exists. He went on to suggest that the word 'know' can be justified only for "mathematically demonstrated and empirically established truths." On Page 15 of his book *HOW TO THINK ABOUT GOD,* Adler writes:

> If argument, reasoning, or inference leads us to affirm the existence of God because we have thereby found tenable reasons for doing so, should we say that we *know* that God exists or that we *believe* it? If the tenable reasons we have found fall short of the degree of certitude that justifies us in using the word "know" for *mathematically demonstrated and empirically established truths,* then we must have recourse to the word "believe," always remembering to add the qualification that the belief we have adopted differs from religious belief in that the truth thus affirmed is affirmed on the basis of reason alone. [Emphasis is mine.]

Adler's demand for empirically established truths is well justified. This is exactly what I hope you will find here, presented in the next few chapters.

The combined usage of scriptural material and established scientific facts has produced the first physical evidence not only that God exists, but also that He is indeed the omnipotent, omniscient, and omnipresent deity who created the universe. And that He continues to run and sustain it.

RELATIVE IMPORTANCE OF GOD'S CREATIONS

One of the significant products of combining scripture and science is an emerging picture of God's identity. Before we can grasp this emerging picture, we need first to reflect on God's works—His creations. At this stage of human history, we have acquired a tremendous wealth of knowledge about ourselves and the universe we live in. The following established facts are readily available to the general public.

Our solar system spans distances of up to 8,000,000,000 miles. The sun is 93,000,000 miles away from our planet Earth, and its light reaches us in approximately eight minutes. From the border of our solar system, the planet Earth with its mean diameter of about 8,000 miles, is relatively minute.

Our sun is one of a billion trillion stars known to exist in our universe. The sun, however, is one of the 'dim' stars. A 'bright' star is one million times as bright as our sun. Yet, on a clear day, one can be overwhelmed (and well sunburned) by the amount of energy radiated by this 'dim' star.

Our sun is only one of perhaps two hundred billion stars within our galaxy, the Milky Way. The size of the Milky Way is awesome. It would take us 100,000 years at the speed of light to cross it from one end to the other. Bearing in mind that the sun's light travels 93,000,000 miles in eight minutes, we can get a sense of the vastness of the Milky Way—a hundred thousand light years across.

From the outer limit of our galaxy, how significant is the planet Earth? Without any self-emitted light, how visible is it from that spot? Even if we employed the most powerful telescope in existence today, we could not see the Earth from the outer limits of our own galaxy.

While we are still in our galaxy, our planet is already diminished to invisibility. If we reduced the size of our galaxy to the area of this page, the dot at the end of this sentence would be much larger than our whole solar system. Recalling that the solar system spans distances of 8,000,000,000 miles, the 8,000-mile wide planet Earth is somewhere within this dot.

Our 'next-door' neighbor galaxy, or the closest similar galaxy to our Milky Way, is 2,000,000 light years away. If we go to the center of this neighboring galaxy, can you visualize the planet Earth? How significant is it from *that* distance?

By moving from our galaxy to the nearest galaxy, we are already talking about incredible distances, millions of light years. Yet, our universe contains a vast number of galaxies.

Back in the 1950's, Donald Shane and Carl Wirtanen drew the first map of the universe and its galaxies. One thousand galaxies were surveyed then. Since the drawing of that first map, scientists have discovered one billion (1,000,000,000) galaxies, more than a million times what Shane and Wirtanen reported some forty years ago.

In our imaginary journey from one galaxy to the next, we have spanned distances of millions of light years. We are now talking about billions of light years within our universe; as many as 26,000,000,000 light years. Have you lost track of our planet Earth? How significant is it within the universe?

It is very important to keep the size and significance of our planet in perspective in order to appreciate the relative significance of tiny creatures who inhabited this planet for a brief period of time, but were exalted by others to the status of God.

> *When I behold your heavens, the work of your fingers.*
> *The moon and stars which you set in place—*
> *What is man that you should be mindful of him,*
> *or the son of man that you should care for him?*
> **[Psalm 8:4-5]**

SEVEN UNIVERSES!

Now, we receive a real shock; according to scriptural sources, our universe is the smallest and innermost of seven universes!

Multiple universes are frequently mentioned in the Bible:

*Think! The heavens, even the highest heavens,
the heavens of the heavens,
belong to the Lord, your God,
as well as the earth and everything on it.*
> **[Deuteronomy 10:14]**

*Yet who is really able to build him a house,
since the heavens and even the highest heavens
cannot contain him?*
> **[2 Chronicles 2:5]**

*You kingdoms of the earth, sing to God,
chant praise to the Lord who rides
on the heights of the ancient heavens.
Behold his voice resounds, the voice of power:
"Confess the power of God!"*
> **[Psalm 68:33-35]**

In the above verses from the Old Testament, we note that there are 'heavens' and 'heavens of heavens' or 'the highest heavens.' In the New Testament we find an interesting reference to the third heaven:

*I know a man in Christ who, fourteen years ago,
whether he was in or outside his body I cannot say,
only God can say—a man who was snatched up to the third heaven.
I know that this man—whether in or outside his body I do not know,
God knows—was snatched up to Paradise...*
> **[2 Corinthians 12:2-4]**

The creation of seven universes is spelled out in the Quran. The picture drawn is that of seven universes in layers, one inside the other like seven elliptical balls:

*God is the one who created seven universes, in layers.
You will never see a flaw in the creation of the Most High.
Keep looking!
Do you see any flaw?*
> **[Quran 67:3]**

God is the one who created for you everything on earth,
and He perfected in the sky seven universes.
He is fully aware of all things.
[Quran 2:29]

THE GREATNESS OF GOD

The diameter of our universe, the smallest and innermost of the seven universes, encompasses distances of some 26,000,000,000 light years. This number equals 153 billion trillions of miles (153,000,000,000,000,000 miles).

Within the circumference of our universe, there are a billion trillion stars (not even counting the uncountable decillions of other heavenly bodies). It would take us 32 billion years just to count one quintillion of these stars, at the rate of one star per second. This is simply counting them, not creating them!

Can you imagine the circumference of our universe? Can you envision a circumference surrounding distances of 26,000,000,000 light years? Considering our universe to be first, the second universe is necessarily larger than our universe. In view of the enormous vastness of our 'small' universe, the size of the third universe, which surrounds two universes is already incomprehensible. How about the fourth universe; or the fifth; or the sixth; or the seventh?

Now comes another shock; in order to give us an approximation of His profoundly awesome greatness, God tells us that He is holding the seven universes within the fist of His hand!

They never valued God as He should be valued.
The whole Earth will be within His fist on the Day of Resurrection;
in fact, all the universes are contained within His right hand.
He is the Most Magnificent, the Most High;
far above anything they idolize.
[Quran 39:67]

OTHER EXPRESSIONS OF HIS GREATNESS
The scriptures are full of verses expressing God's greatness, His infinite power and knowledge:

...Great is the Lord and highly to be praised;
and awesome is he, beyond all gods.
For all the gods of the nations are things of nought,
but the Lord made the heavens.
Splendor and majesty go before him;
praise and joy are in his holy place.
Give to the Lord, you families of nations,
give to the Lord glory and praise;
give to the Lord the glory due his name!
Bring gifts, and enter his presence;
worship the Lord in holy attire.
Tremble before him, all the earth;
he has made the world firm, not to be moved.
Let the heavens be glad and the earth rejoice;
let them say among the nations: The Lord is king.
[I Chronicles 16:25-31]

He stretches out the North over empty space,
and suspends the earth over nothing at all;
He binds up the waters in his clouds,
yet the cloud is not rent by their weight;
He holds back the appearance of the full moon
by spreading his clouds before it.
He has marked out a circle on the surface
of the deep as the boundary of light and darkness.
The pillars of the heavens tremble and
are stunned at his thunderous rebuke.
[Job 26:7-11]

Lo, God is great beyond our knowledge;
the number of his years is past searching out.
[Job 36:26]

By the word of the Lord the heavens were made;
by the breath of his mouth all their host.
He gathers the waters of the sea as in a flask;
in cellars he confines the deep.
Let all the earth fear the Lord;
let all who dwell in the world revere him.
For he spoke, and it was made;
he commanded, and it stood forth.
[Psalm 33:6-9]

The heavens declare the glory of God,
and the firmament proclaims his handiwork.
Day pours out of the word to day,
and the night to night imparts knowledge;
Not a word nor a discourse whose voice is not heard;
Through all the earth their voice resounds,
and to the ends of the world, their message.
[Psalm 19:2-5]

At the outer limit of the largest, outermost universe, the planet Earth is reduced to an infinitesimally minute speck. If the Earth, or if the whole solar system and all its contents suddenly vanished, how much of a loss would that be in God's dominion?

GOD'S OMNIPOTENCE & OMNISCIENCE

The scriptures emphasize that the greatness of God is not merely in size, but in the fact that He is aware of and controls all of our affairs:

To him who rises without assurance of his life
he gives safety and support.
He sustains the mighty by his strength,
and his eyes are on their ways.
[Job 24:22-23]

God reveals to us that He is fully aware of even the smallest detail in the universe. In the Gospel of Matthew, for example, Jesus tells us that *"every hair of your head has been counted"*:

*[Jesus said,] "Do not fear those who deprive the body
of life but cannot destroy the soul.
Rather, fear him who can destroy both body
and soul in Gehenna.
Are not two sparrows sold for next to nothing?
Yet not a single sparrow falls to the ground without
your Father's consent.
As for you, every hair of your head has been counted;
so do not be afraid of anything..."*
[Matthew 10:28-31]

*Jesus fixed his gaze on them and said,
"For man it is impossible but not for God,
with God all things are possible."*
[Mark 10:27]

The idea of God's omniscience and omnipresence is also clear in the Book of Psalms:

*From heaven the Lord looks down;
he sees all mankind.
From his fixed throne he beholds all who dwell on the earth.
He who fashioned the heart of each,
he who knows all their works.*
[Psalm 33:13-15]

God's control of our *"inmost thoughts"* and of our affairs is described by Mary in the Gospel of Luke:

*"God who is mighty has done great things for me,
holy is his name;
His mercy is from age to age on those who fear him.
He has shown might with his arm;
he has confused the proud in their inmost thoughts.
He has deposed the mighty from their thrones
and raised the lowly to high places."*
[Luke 1:49-52]

With Him are the keys to all secrets;
none knows them except He.
He knows everything on land and in the sea.
Not a leaf falls without His knowledge.
Nor is there a grain in the depths of the soil,
be it wet or dry, that is not recorded in a profound record.
[Quran 6:59]

"Not a sparrow falls to the ground without God's consent" and every hair is counted, every seed recorded. In fact, even the perpetual motion of the sub-atomic components of the very ink and paper you are looking at is controlled by God. This sub-atomic control is indirectly implied in the Bible, but specifically mentioned in the Quran:

Any condition you may be in, any scripture you may read,
indeed, anything you do is never done without us
being witnesses thereof, even as you begin to plan it.
Not a single atom is hidden from your Lord,
be it in the earth, or in the heavens;
not even smaller than an atom, nor larger;
everything is counted and recorded in a profound record.
[Quran 10:61]

Even happiness, that internal feeling of ecstacy, is exclusively controlled by God, regardless of extraneous circumstances. Furthermore, the scripture stipulates that happiness is only temporary for the evildoers, but genuine and everlasting for the righteous children of God. God is the sole controller of our happiness:

I bless the Lord who counsels me;
even in the night my heart exhorts me.
I set the Lord ever before me;
with him at my right hand I shall not be disturbed.
Therefore my heart is glad and my soul rejoices....
[Psalm 16:7-9]

Once, in my security, I said,
"I shall never be disturbed."
O Lord, in your good will you had endowed me

with majesty and strength;
but when you hid your face I was terrified.
[Psalm 30:7-8]

God is the one who makes you happy or sad.
...He is the one who makes you rich or poor.
[Quran 53:43, 48]

CONCLUSION

We learn from the combining of science and the scripture how infinitesimal we are, and how great and infinitely powerful God is. We realize that our finite minds cannot possibly fathom God:

As high as the heavens are above the earth,
so high are My ways above your ways
and My thoughts above your thoughts.
[Isaiah 55:9]

The Quran repeats this same theme:

No visions can ever encompass Him,
while He encompasses all visions....
[Quran 6:103]

Our minds are overwhelmed at the vastness of our universe, let alone the 'infinite' size of the largest, outermost universe. How can we grasp God's greatness when something *"held within His hand"* is beyond our grasp?

Now we are in a better position to appreciate the following statements of His absolute Oneness:

High above all nations is the Lord;
above the heavens is his glory.
Who is like the Lord, our God, who is enthroned on high
and looks upon the heavens and the earth below?
[Psalm 113:4-6]

His Oneness is not only in His glory, but also in the fact that He alone is eternally pre-existing:

> *Proclaim: "He is the only God, the eternal God;*
> *He never begets, nor was He begotten.*
> *There is none that is comparable to Him."*
> **[Quran 112:1-4]**

He alone should be worshiped:
> *I, the Lord, am your God, who brought you out*
> *of the land of Egypt, that place of slavery.*
> *You shall not have other gods besides me.*
> *You shall not carve idols for yourselves*
> *in the shape of anything in the sky above*
> *or on the earth below or in the waters beneath the earth;*
> *you shall not bow down before them or worship them.*
> *For I, the Lord, your God, am a jealous God....*
> **[Exodus 20:2-5]**

His greatness is beyond our comprehension:
> *He is the only God; there is no other god besides Him.*
> *He is the knower of all secrets, as well as all declarations.*
> *He is the Most Gracious, the Most Merciful.*
> *He is the only God; there is no other god besides Him.*
> *He is the King, the Sacred, the Peace-giver, the Faithful,*
> *the Supreme, the Almighty, the Most Powerful, the Most High.*
> *God be glorified; He is much too Great*
> *to have any idols to rank with Him.*
> *He is the only God; there is no god besides Him.*
> *He is the Creator, the Initiator, the Designer.*
> *To Him belongs the most beautiful attributes.*
> *Everything in the heavens and the earth glorifies Him.*
> *He is the Almighty, the Most Wise.*
> **[Quran 59:22-24]**

Truly, this is the one whom we should worship with all our minds and all our souls and all our hearts!

Chapter Nine

JESUS: SEARCH FOR PROVEN HISTORY

> *[Jesus] said, "I am a servant of God;*
> *who has decreed that I shall be given the scripture;*
> *He has appointed me a prophet;*
> *and bestowed His blessings upon me*
> *wherever I might be; and enjoined me to observe*
> *the contact prayers, and the giving of alms,*
> *for as long as I live, and to honor my mother.*
> *He made me not an evil tyrant.*
> *Peace is my lot the day I was born,*
> *the day I die, and the day I am resurrected."*
> *This is the truthful story of Jesus, the son of Mary,*
> *about whom they still conjecture.*
> **[Quran 19:30-34]**

At the root of Christian doctrine is the question of the identity of Jesus Christ of Nazareth. We have already examined the concepts of Jesus as God, the son of God, part of the Trinity and the redeemer of mankind. In all cases we have seen major flaws in these traditional concepts of this man. Now, however, there is something new which will open exciting new doors in our search: the first physical evidence to validate all relevant aspects of Jesus' history.

Something new has recently emerged in the spiritual world; it is no longer purely spiritual. An unexpected source has been found which authenticates the scripture. The result is that we now possess documents that are proven to be divine revelation.

AUTHENTICATING MATHEMATICAL CODE

An intricate mathematical code, far beyond the ability of human intelligence, has been discovered imbedded in the fabric of the scripture. Like an ancient time capsule, it remained hidden until our knowledge grew sophisticated enough to decode its intricacies. This code was deciphered by computers.

The discovery of mathematically coded scripture assures us that the verses, words, letters and all parameters of the *original* scripture were written down in accordance with an intricate pattern that is clearly superhuman.

The first indication of this mathematical composition was in the 11th century by Rabbi Judah the Pious. In a book entitled *STUDIES IN JEWISH MYSTICISM* (Association for Jewish Studies, 1982, p. 91), Joseph Dan writes that Rabbi Judah and his disciples developed a theory that:

> ...the words and letters of the various prayers are not accidental, nor are they only vehicles for their literal meaning. Their order, especially their numbers, reflect a mystical harmony, a sacred divine rhythm. This mystical harmony can be discovered in historical events, directed by God; in nature, especially in the miraculous occurrences directly influenced by divine powers; and first and foremost, in the Bible. According to Rabbi Judah and the Ashkenazi Hasidic school in general, there can be nothing accidental in the Bible, not even the forms of letters, the punctuation, the vocalization, and especially—in the numerical structures—the number of certain letters, consonants or vowels in a certain verse; the number of words from the same root; the number and variety of divine names in a certain pericope, the absence of one or more letters from a chapter, and many other elements of the Scriptures besides their content.

Nine centuries after Rabbi Judah stated these elements of the code, the computer has demonstrated each of them. As detailed in this chapter and the next, the original scripture was mathematically composed in a way that encodes and guards every single one of its parameters. If the scripture were tampered with, the code would be broken.

Joseph Dan writes that Rabbi Judah was critical of the French and British Jews when they altered the morning prayer by adding a few words (Ibid., p. 88). Rabbi Judah pointed out that such an addition destroys the numerical structure of the prayer and renders it utterly nullified. He maintained that it is the "numerical combination," rather than the "meanings" of the words that effects the needed contact between the worshiper and God. Even the specific, nineteen-based, numerical system of the scripture was reported by Rabbi Judah:

> The people [Jews] in France made it a custom to add [in the morning prayer] the words: " *'Ashrei temimei derekh* [blessed are those who walk the righteous way]," and our Rabbi, the Pious, of blessed memory, wrote that they were completely and utterly wrong. It is all gross falsehood, because there are only nineteen times that the Holy Name is mentioned [in that portion of the morning prayer] ...and similarly you find the word *'Elohim* nineteen times in the pericope of *Ve-'elleh shemot*.... Similarly, you find that Israel is called "sons" nineteen times, and there are many other examples. All these sets of nineteen are intricately intertwined, and they contain many secrets and esoteric meanings, which are contained in more than eight large volumes. Therefore, anyone who has the fear of God in him will not listen to the words of the Frenchmen who add the verse *"'Ashrei temimei derekh," and blessed are the righteous who walk in the paths of God's Torah*, for according to their additions the Holy Name is mentioned twenty times...and this is a great mistake.
>
> Furthermore, in this section there are 152 words (152 = 19 x 8) but if you add *"'Ashrei temimei derekh"* there are 158 words. This is nonsense, for it is a great and hidden secret why there should be 152 words...but it cannot be explained in a short treatise. ...In order to understand this religious phenomenon, we have to take the basic contention of this treatise exactly as it is stated: every addition or omission of a word, or even of a single letter, from the sacred text of the prayers destroys the religious meaning of the prayer as a whole and

is to be regarded as a grave sin, a sin which could result in eternal exile for those who commit it....
>   (*STUDIES IN JEWISH MYSTICISM*, pp. 88-89)

WHAT DOES IT MEAN?

The discovery of numerical structures within the scriptures and the divinely instituted liturgies have resulted in a number of important conclusions. Some of these conclusions appear in *STUDIES IN JEWISH MYSTICISM* (Ibid., p. 92):

> (1) No change can be tolerated in the text of the prayers, not even a minute one, because every change — even of one letter — would destroy the numerical harmony inherent in the text....
>
> (2) The liturgy received new importance and new meaning within the framework of religious practice. A completely new dimension was added in this way to the daily prayer service; it stopped being just a reciting of requests and praises of God in ancient formulas, and became a vehicle for becoming a participant in a mystical, divine harmony. The prayers suddenly received a new depth of meaning and importance, which was undreamed of in the thousand years that had passed since they were formulated.

Joseph Dan reports that "the fierce polemical tone of Rabbi Judah's criticism of the changes introduced by the 'Frenchmen' in the prayers can therefore be explained as a result of his fear that the prayers may be regarded as completely human in origin and meaning, making them secular and meaningless in religious and mystical practices." Rabbi Judah was also fearful that changes to the prayer would disrupt the mystical dimension and break the connection with God that they created:

> According to him [Rabbi Judah], even if the context and meaning of the prayer is religious, expressing love and devotion to God, it still will be just "a secular song like that of the non-Jews" if it does not have the added mystical dimension of hidden truth [the mathematical composition], which cannot be revealed by the literal meaning of the words alone. In his polemic, Rabbi Judah does not defend only the specific tradition of prayer which he received from his parents and teachers; he also defends prayer as an elevating force, forming a connection

between man and God, a connection that no mere words can achieve.
(*STUDIES IN JEWISH MYSTICISM*, pp. 92-93)

The divinely instituted liturgies, in their original, unaltered words, are so numerically composed that they can be compared to the combination of a locked safe; we need to dial that specific combination to establish contact with our creator. This is probably why the daily prayers were called in Jesus' language SLA and in Arabic SALA which means "contact" or "connection."

Because of this understanding, Rabbi Judah warned his neighbors in France and England that if they allowed any change in the text of the prayers, their prayers would become "like the songs of the uncircumcised non-Jews." Free expression of feelings, religious or secular, was regarded by Rabbi Judah as a non-Jewish song, which has no place in the framework of worship. Obviously, the slightest change, even of one letter, would destroy the divinely composed numerical system and thus, the "combination" to open the lock and establish contact with God would not work.

IMPORTANCE TO OUR SUBJECT

The discovery of mathematically authenticated scripture provides a totally unexpected opportunity to explore the validity of the Christian understanding of Jesus. If there were a scripture which was proven to be unaltered by human beings, it would give us a safe point of reference for our study.

The idea of mathematically composing a literary work is certainly novel to human thinking, and unique to the scriptures. The numerical pattern serves both as an authenticating tool and as a guard to protect and preserve the scripture. Obviously, finding original, unaltered scripture is of crucial importance. The slightest change in the text of a mathematically coded literary work would disrupt or utterly destroy such a code; the mathematical pattern would simply disappear. As pointed out by Rabbi Judah, "every addition or omission of a word, or even of a single letter...destroys the religious meaning of the prayer as a whole and is regarded as a grave sin." From a purely mathematical point of view, the slightest change renders the pattern non-existent; 76, for example, is a multiple of 19, but 77 or 75 is not.

ORIGINAL SCRIPTURE

There is proof that one scripture is completely intact, and perfectly preserved. Unlike other known scriptures, this one still exists in its original, untranslated language—just as it was revealed 1400 years ago. It is known to be complete, with no loss of any of the original revelation.

Western access to this scripture has been limited by the fact that the people to whom it was originally delivered have all but buried it with their cultural tradition. They believe that it is the basis of their religious belief, when in fact, what they practice generally goes contrary to its teachings. This scripture is the Quran.

In a recent translation of the Quran, the translator emphasizes the role of the number nineteen as an authenticating code for the Quran. In 1968, through computer decoding, and totally independent of the work of Rabbi Judah the Pious, Dr. Rashad Khalifa discovered that an extremely intricate 19-based numerical structure encodes and guards every aspect of the Quran.

In the second edition of his translation *QURAN: THE FINAL TESTAMENT* (Islamic Productions, 1989), Khalifa refers to Rabbi Judah's work, and suggests that nineteen represents God's own signature on everything He created. He also provides the first plausible explanation for the prominence of the 19-based mathematical pattern throughout the scriptures, as well as the universe. In his appendix entitled *"19: The Creator's Signature"* (Ibid., p. 709) Khalifa writes:

> The scriptures are not the only mathematically composed creations of God where the number 19 is the common denominator. It is profound indeed that Galileo made his famous statement: "Mathematics is the language with which God created the universe." A plethora of scientific findings have now shown that the number 19 represents God's signature upon certain creations. This divine stamp appears throughout the universe in much the same manner as the signatures of Michelangelo and Picasso identify their works. For example:

1. The sun, the moon, and the earth become aligned in the same relative positions once every 19 years (see the *ENCYCLOPEDIA JUDAICA* under "Calendar").

2. Halley's comet, a profound heavenly phenomenon, visits our solar system every 76 years, 19x4.

3. God's stamp on you and me is manifested in the fact that the human body contains 209 bones, 19x11.

4. *LANGMAN'S MEDICAL EMBRYOLOGY*, by T. W. Sadler, is used as a textbook in most of the Medical Schools in the U.S.A. On Page 88 of the Fifth edition, we read the following statement: "In general the length of pregnancy for a full term fetus is considered to be 280 days or 40 weeks after onset of the last menstruation, or more accurately, 266 days or 38 weeks after fertilization." The numbers 266 and 38 are both multiples of 19.

SPECIFIC RELEVANCE

As in other research, if we can find an authenticated outside source we have a good yardstick against which to measure the other information we have about Jesus Christ and Christian doctrine. As demonstrated by the number of quotes in previous chapters, the Quran speaks a great deal about Jesus and about specific Christian doctrines. Once we are convinced that the Quran is indeed an intact divine revelation we have an invaluable tool in our research.

Thus, when the mathematically coded statements of the Quran say, for example, that *"Jesus created live birds from clay"* (Quran 3:49 and 5:110), this becomes a proven statement by virtue of its mathematically authenticated composition.

After reviewing the intricate mathematical code of the Quran, you will see that we have God's own testimony concerning the history of Jesus; an eyewitness account. The next chapter gives a detailed summary of this unique mathematical code.

> *This is the truthful story of Jesus, the son of Mary, about whom they still conjecture.* **[Quran 19:34]**

Chapter Ten

THE PHYSICAL EVIDENCE

The fool says in his heart, "There is no God."
Such are corrupt; they do abominable deeds;
there is not one who does good.
The Lord looks down from heaven
upon the children of men,
to see if there be one who is wise and seeks God.
All alike have gone astray....
                           [Psalm 14:1-3]

Mathematical composition of a literary work is a totally new concept, though we now realize it has existed for centuries in sacred writings. Since it is a new concept, a brief explanation may be of help.

MATHEMATICALLY COMPOSED LITERATURE
Suppose you are asked to write a book with the stipulation that:

1. Chapter 3 is to contain exactly 532 of the letter 'S'.
2. Chapter 8 is to contain exactly 209 B's, and 779 T's.
3. Chapter 6 is to contain exactly 133 of the letter combination 'ING.'
4. And the total number of sentences must be exactly 57,152.

You will then try to write this hypothetical book, carefully counting and keeping track of those letters and the number of sentences in order to conform with the specifications given to you. As you conform to these specifications, you must write down words and sentences that make sense and tell the reader something important having to do with the subject of your book. This is a simple example of mathematical composition.

These specifications can be increased or decreased to create varying degrees of complexity. The specific counts of certain letters, numbers of specific phrases, numbers of sentences and totals of verse numbers can soon become so interlocking that it becomes virtually impossible to compose such a book.

CODED SCRIPTURE

Mathematically composed liturgies were reported by Rabbi Judah the Pious in the 11th century. To my knowledge, a recent analysis of the Torah has not been done to see if this code is still intact in the entire scripture, but we have already discussed indications that there have been some alterations in the Torah, at the very least in reference to the sons of Abraham. These alterations would have seriously disrupted the code.

The Gospels have been shown to have many problems in their transmission to us. In their present form, they are not good candidates at all for such an analysis.

The Quran, which was revealed in A.D. 610-630, is the only scripture that is known to still exist in its original language, and form. It is also the only book known to be mathematically coded throughout.

All the parameters of the Quran—the numbers and sequences of chapters; the number of verses; the numbers assigned to each verse; the number of words; the number of certain specified letters; the number of words from the same root; the number and variety of divine names; the absence of one or more letters from a word, verse or chapter; the unique and often strange spellings of certain crucial words; and many other elements—are all authenticated by its mathematical code.

HOW IT WAS DISCOVERED
How was this code discovered in the Quran?

Before we can answer that question we need to know a little about a unique feature in Quran—a phenomenon not found in any other literature. Twenty-nine chapters of the Quran are prefixed with certain letters of the Arabic alphabet, or 'Quranic Initials.' Ever since the Quran was revealed more than 14 centuries ago, Muslim and orientalist scholars have been trying to decipher the meaning and possible significance of these mysterious Quranic initials, but to no avail. They remained a mystery to all.

Finally, a Muslim scientist and computer expert named Rashad Khalifa entered the Quran into the computer in hopes of finding some pattern which would explain these initials. Khalifa, a Ph.D. chemist, later on the roster of scientists called 'Technical Assistance Experts' with the United Nations Industrial Development Organization (UNIDO), began his computer study as part of the research for his translation of the Quran into English. The result of his extensive research was the discovery of an intricate mathematical system which pervades the whole Quran and governs every possible parameter, including its initials.

Dr. Khalifa's discovery is extremely significant, especially since it matches the findings of Rabbi Judah the Pious. The common denominator of the Quran's mathematical code, the number *nineteen,* was reported by Rabbi Judah "in the liturgy, in the Scripture, in nature, in historical events and throughout the universe."

Thus, God's 'signature,' the number *nineteen,* encodes and guarantees every letter and every parameter of the Quran, and intact portions of the Torah. It also places the Creator's stamp on our own creation, on major historical events, on the sun/moon/earth interactions and throughout the universe.

WESTERN KNOWLEDGE OF THE CODE

Why haven't you heard about this? Here in the West, Rashad Khalifa's work has not received the attention it deserves. Only two 'Western' comments on his momentous discovery are noteworthy. The first comment appeared in the *SCIENTIFIC AMERICAN* of September 1980. Martin Gardner wrote of Khalifa's initial publication in the West:

I later discovered that the author of this monograph, Rashad Khalifa, is an Egyptian who received a doctorate in biochemistry from an American university, where he also taught for a time. His monograph was published privately in the U.S. in 1972.... Dr. Khalifa's monograph attempts to show that *19* appears throughout the Koran too often to be there by chance. The number of suras in the Koran is 114, a multiple of *19*. A famous verse called the Basmala ("In the name of Allah, most gracious, most merciful"), which opens every sura but one, has *19* letters. Its first word (ism) appears *19* times in the Koran. The second word (Allah) is found 2,698, or 142 x *19*, times. The number of times the third word (al-Rahman) appears is 57, which is also a multiple of *19*, as is the number of times the fourth word (al-Raheem) appears, 114.

It's an ingenious study of the Quran, but it could have been more impressive if Khalifa had consulted me before he wrote it. *Nineteen* is an unusual prime. For example, it's the sum of the first powers of 9 and 10 and the difference between the second powers of 9 and 10.
(*Scientific American*, Sept. 1980, p. 22)

Three years later the Canadian Council on the Study of Religion reported in its *QUARTERLY REVIEW* of April 1983 that the code Khalifa discovered is "an authenticating proof of the divine origin of the Quran."

Since 1983, little notice has been taken of this work. In spite of that, Dr. Khalifa's work has been published in the United States in six books:

1. *MIRACLE OF THE QURAN: Significance of the Mysterious Alphabets*, Islamic Productions, St. Louis, Missouri, 1973.

2. *THE COMPUTER SPEAKS: God's Message to the World*, Renaissance Productions, Tucson, Arizona, 1981.

3. *QUR'AN: The Final Scripture*, Islamic Productions, Tucson, Arizona, 1981.

4. *QURAN: VISUAL PRESENTATION OF THE MIRACLE*, Ibid, 1982.

5. *QUR'AN, HADITH AND ISLAM*, Ibid, 1982.

6. *QURAN: The Final Testament*, Ibid, 1989.

MIDEASTERN KNOWLEDGE OF THE CODE

In the Middle East, the story is a little different. Beginning in the late sixties, this work received wide publicity throughout the Islamic world, rendering Khalifa's name a household word. By the end of 1973, Rashad Khalifa had become a popular hero, commanding full-house audiences as he lectured at the universities, mosques, organizations, and even royal and presidential palaces.

However, his discovery led to unavoidable conclusions which ran contrary to certain basic beliefs of the traditional Muslim clergy. These conclusions boil down to a total rejection of the 'Islamic traditions' which have been added onto the religion over the centuries, and a return to the pure teachings of Quran alone. Consequently, Khalifa's popularity was reversed and his life threatened in a number of Muslim countries.

Before Khalifa incurred the wrath of the Muslim clergy, many popular magazines and newspapers in the Middle East, from Morocco to Pakistan, reported his discoveries. Millions of summaries in pamphlet and bulletin form are still secretly circulating among the Muslims of the world.

Khalifa's first publicized report appeared in the most popular magazine of the Middle East, Egypt's *AKHERSA* (January 24, 1973). Updates of his research were subsequently published by the same magazine (November 28, 1973 and December 31, 1975). Many other magazines and newspaper articles by and about Khalifa appeared throughout the world in many languages.

Then, very early in the morning on January 31, 1990, Rashad Khalifa's life was taken by one or more assassins who had broken into his office in Tucson, Arizona, and waited for him. There is no doubt that his life was taken in an attempt to stem the growing rejection of distorted Islamic tradition and a return to the Quran alone—a movement which he spearheaded.

DETAILS INTRODUCED

The relevance of the Quran's mathematical code to the history of Jesus makes it necessary to review this code in some detail. The Quran was recorded as it was revealed—in fragments which were separated in both time and place, and positioned like the pieces of a jigsaw puzzle into the final scripture. Since the order of revelation is different from the order of final position, two consecutive verses may be separated by as much as two years and 300 miles according to their chronological revelation.

Before his assassination, Dr. Khalifa graciously gave me permission to reproduce as much of the appendix covering the mathematical code as I wished from his translation, *QURAN: THE FINAL TESTAMENT* (First Edition, Islamic Productions, 1989). I have chosen to pick out the simpler facts to summarize here, but have summarized his entire appendix as an appendix to this book.

THE CODE — SIMPLE FACTS

Though the code was initially discovered by examining the occurrences of Quranic initials in the initialed chapters of Quran, there is a large number of much less complex parameters to the code. Here is a brief listing of some of them:

1. There are 114 chapters in the Quran, or 19 x 6.

2. The total number of verses in the Quran is 6346, or 19 x 334.

3. Then you add the 30 different numbers which are mentioned in the Quran's text (i.e. one God, two brothers, etc.), the total is 162146 or 19 x 8534.

4. The first statement in Quran, "In the name of God, Most Gracious, Most Merciful" consists of 19 Arabic letters. Known as the *'Basmalah'*, it prefaces every chapter except Chapter 9.

5. Though missing from Chapter 9, exactly 19 chapters later the *Basmalah* occurs twice. Chapter 27 has this statement at its beginning and in verse 30. This makes the total number of times the *Basmalah* occurs in the Quran 114, or 19 x 6.

6. Since there are 19 chapters between the missing *Basmalah* and the extra one, the sum of those chapter numbers is a multiple of 19. (The sum of any 19 consecutive numbers is a multiple of 19.) But the total, 342, is also the exact number of words between the two occurrences of the *Basmalah* in Chapter 27. This number, 342, is 19 x 18.

7. Every word in the *Basmalah* occurs throughout the Quran a number of times which is a multiple of 19.

8. The very first revelation that was given to the prophet of Islam, Mohammed, came as 19 words.

9. The total number of letters making up the 19 words of the first revelation is 76, 19 x 4.

10. Though they were the first revelation, these verses are placed at the beginning of Chapter 96. This chapter is atop the last 19 chapters.

11. Chapter 96 consists of 304 Arabic letters, or 19 x 16.

12. The last chapter revealed (Chapter 110) has 19 words, and its first verse is 19 letters.

13. God's name in Arabic, *'Allah,'* occurs in the Quran 2698 times, or 19 x 142.

14. If you add the numbers of the verses where *'Allah'* occurs, the total is 118123 or 19 x 6217.

15. The main message in the Quran is that there is only One God. The number of times that the word 'one' is used to refer to this concept of One God is 19.

16. The word 'Quran' occurs in 38 different chapters, or 19 x 2.

17. The total number of times 'the Quran' is mentioned is 57, 19 x 3.

18. Within the 114 chapters of the Quran, 29 of them begin with the Quranic initials discussed earlier. Intermixed between the first initialed chapter (Chapter 2) and the last initialed chapter (Chapter 68) are 38 non-initialed chapters, or 19 x 2.

19. In that same group of chapters, from Chapter 2 to Chapter 68, there are 19 alternating sets of initialed and non-initialed chapters.
20. The total number of verses making up this group of chapters is 5263, 19 x 277.
21. Within this group of chapters there are also 2641 occurrences of the word 'Allah', or 19 x 139. Of course, that leaves 57, or 19 x 4, occurrences of that word outside of this group.
22. If you add the chapter and verse numbers of the 57 occurrences of 'Allah' outside the initialed section, the total is 2432 or 19 x 128.
23. There are a large number of discoveries having to do with the numbers of the chapters and verses. Many of them are very complex and interrelated. Here is a simple one to give you a feel for these discoveries: If you add the numbers assigned to all the chapters, plus the numbers assigned to all of the verses, plus the number of verses in the Quran, the total is 346199 or 19 x 19 x 959.
24. If you look at the initialed chapters separately and add the chapter numbers, verse numbers and number of verses, the total is 190133, 19 x 10007. Of course it follows that the total for the uninitialed chapters, 156066, is also divisible by 19.

There are a great many more discoveries, most of them more complex than the ones presented above. Additional discoveries continue to be made as Dr. Khalifa's work is carried on by the many students of pure Quran he left behind.

You may already be convinced that this interlocking occurrence of the number 19 is too frequent to be accidental. If not, the next section dealing with the Quranic initials should dispel your doubts.

QURANIC INITIALS

As we discussed earlier in this chapter, it was the search for an explanation of the Quranic Initials which led to the discovery of the code imbedded in the Arabic text of this scripture. These initials exhibit many aspects of the code, when looked at as individual sets and when looked at as a whole.

Let us begin by looking at the initials which use a single letter. The first one we will examine is the initial which has the English transliteration of 'Q'.

THE INITIAL 'Q.' (Qaaf)
There are several special phenomena having to do with the initial Q. Perhaps it can be seen as standing for Quran. This is especially so since there are two Q-initialed chapters, each with 57 (19 x 3) Q's in them. Thus, the total of Q's in both chapters is 114 (19 x 6), the same number as the number of chapters in the Quran.

The fact that both Q-initialed chapters contain exactly 57 Q's is quite remarkable because the first of them (Chapter 42) is more than twice as long as the second (Chapter 50).

There is another remarkable phenomenon in the sum of the number of each chapter with the number of verses in that chapter. Chapter 42 has 53 verses; 42 plus 53 is 95, 19 x 5. If we look at the other Q-initialed chapter, 50, it has 45 verses; 50 plus 45 is also 95.

THE INITIAL 'N.' (Noon)
This initial prefixes only one chapter, number 68. The total number of occurrences of N in this chapter is 133, or 19 x 7.

THE INITIAL 'Š.' (Saad)
Š prefixes three different chapters, 7, 19 and 38. The total occurrences of Š in these three chapters taken together is 152, or 19 x 8.

Most of the time the initials occur together in sets. Next, we will examine some of these sets.

THE INITIALS 'Y.S.' (Ya Seen)
These two initials are found at the beginning of Chapter 36. The number of times that these two letters appear in this chapter is 285, or 19 x 15.

THE INITIALS 'H.M.' (Haa Meem)
This set of initials is found initializing the seven consecutive chapters 40 through 46. The total occurrence of these two in all of these chapters is 2147, or 19 x 113.

THE INITIALS 'Á.S.Q.' (Ayn Seen Qaf)
Chapter 42 is the only chapter with a set of initials (H.M.) in the first verse and another (Á.S.Q.) in verse two. The number of times the letters of this second set of initials are in Chapter 42 is 209, or 19 x 11.

CONCLUSION
There are more sets of initials which we could discuss. All of them exhibit similar phenomena to those we have examined. Much more detail is contained in the appendix of this book.

From this short presentation, it is easy to see that the substitution or removal of any word containing one of the initials in an initialed chapter would break the code in that chapter. As the initials become more complex, the difficulty of writing readable and meaningful sentences increases. In some cases the only way that the code could have been written into the Quran was for the language to have been invented around it!

The patterns exhibited in the initialed chapters added to the simpler parameters discussed earlier make an awesome network of coding which pervades the very fabric of the Quran. All this clearly required divine control.

Having established the Quran as a valid outside source, let us continue to examine what we know about Jesus and his teachings.

Chapter Eleven

VIRGIN BIRTH

Upon arriving, the angel said to her:
"Rejoice, O highly favored daughter!
The Lord is with you.
Blessed are you among women."
She was deeply troubled by his words,
and wondered what his greeting meant.
The angel went on to say to her:
"Do not fear, Mary. You have found favor
with God. You shall conceive and
bear a son and give him the name Jesus.
Great will be his dignity...."
                    [Luke 1:28-32]

In today's scientific era many, if not most people are skeptical about the virgin birth of Jesus. Such a miraculous conception is more than they can accept. This doubt is strengthened by the fact that in the Bible Joseph is called Jesus' father. Also, it is only through Joseph that Jesus has a legitimate claim to the line of David, the family line from which the Messiah was to come. Mary was from the line of Levi, and only Joseph tied back to David.

Some, like University of Detroit professor Jane Schaberg, have gone so far as to claim that Jesus was illegitimately conceived. (See Schaberg's book, *THE ILLEGITIMACY OF JESUS*, Harper and Row, 1987.)

Of all aspects of Christian doctrine, the virgin birth is perhaps the most difficult for people to accept. Yet it is confirmed by the Quran's mathematical code.

The story of Jesus' ancestry and birth is prominently narrated in the Quran. It is well established by the scriptures that Jesus was a descendant of Aaron, who was the brother of Moses. Aaron and Moses' father, Amram, head of the Amramite tribe, is given such an important position in the Quran that its third chapter is named *'The Amramites.'*

MARY

When Mary's mother conceived her, she dedicated the baby in her womb to the service of God. We learn from the Quran that she was rather disappointed when the baby turned out to be a girl. Nevertheless, she prayed that God might accept her newborn daughter:

> *The Amramite woman said, "My Lord,*
> *I dedicate the fruit of my womb to your service.*
> *Please accept this offer from me;*
> *You are the Hearer, the Omniscient."*
> *When she gave birth to her, she said,*
> *"My Lord, I have given birth to a girl;"*
> *God was fully aware of what she bore.*
> *"And the girl is not the same as the boy;*
> *I have named her Mary, and I invoke Your protection for her and her seed from Satan, the rejected."*
> *Her Lord accepted Mary, a gracious acceptance,*
> *and brought her up a gracious upbringing,*
> *and Zachariah was her guardian....*
> **[Quran 3:35-37]**

A similar account is given in the apocryphal book, *The Gospel of the Birth of Mary:*

> *Afterwards the angel appeared to Anna*
> *his (Joachim's) wife saying:*
> *Fear not, neither think that which you see is a spirit.*
> *For I am that angel who hath offered up*

your prayers and alms before God,
and am now sent to you, that I may inform you,
that a daughter will be born unto you, who shall be called Mary,
and shall be blessed above all women....
being an unparalleled instance
without any pollution or defilement,
and a virgin not knowing any man,
shall bring forth a son, who both by his grace
and name and works, shall be the saviour of the world.
[Lost Books of the Bible, 1974, p. 19]

As we see above, the Quran and the Apocrypha both hold Mary in the highest esteem, *"above all women."* In fact, the Quran uses Mary as the prime example of a believer.

This esteem in which the scripture holds Mary is illustrated again below:

Then Mary said: "My being proclaims the greatness of the Lord,
my spirit finds joy in God my savior,
For he has looked upon his servant in her lowliness;
all ages to come shall call me blessed.
God who is mighty has done great things for me, holy is his name;
His mercy is from age to age on those who fear him."
[Luke 1:46-50]

Proclaim that the angels said, "O Mary,
God has chosen you and blessed you;
He has chosen you above all women."
[Quran 3:42]

She [Mary] shall be, immediately upon her birth,
full of the grace of the Lord....
she shall serve the Lord night and day in fasting and prayer,
shall abstain from every unclean thing
and never know any man.
[Lost Books of the Bible, p. 19]

THE VIRGIN BIRTH ACCORDING TO THE QURAN

The virgin birth is clearly indicated in the Quran, where Mary exclaims: *"My Lord, how can I have a son, when **no man has touched me?**":*

> *Proclaim that the angels said,*
> *"O Mary, God sends to you good news;*
> *a word from Him to be called the Messiah, Jesus, the son of Mary.*
> *Great will be his dignity in this world, and,*
> *in the Hereafter, he will be among those close to God.*
> *He will preach to the people while still in the cradle,*
> *as well as when he grows up. He will be righteous."*
> *She said, "My Lord, how can I have a son,*
> *when no man has touched me?"*
> *(The angel) said, "God thus creates whatever He wills.*
> *To have anything done, He simply says to it, 'Be,' and it is."*
> **[Quran 3:45-47]**

The details of the virgin birth are mathematically authenticated in the Quran's Chapter 19, which is appropriately entitled '*Mary*:'

> *Commemorate in the scripture Mary:*
> *She isolated herself from her family to an Eastern location.*
> *While alone in the sanctuary, we sent to her our spirit.*
> *He materialized before her in human form.*
> *She said, "I invoke God's protection from you,*
> *if you do observe God."*
> *He said, "I am your Lord's messenger,*
> *to grant you an immaculate son."*
> *She said, "How can I have a son,*
> ***when no man has touched me, nor was I ever unchaste?"***
> *He said, "Thus says your Lord, 'It is easy for Me.'*
> *We will render him a portent for the people*
> *and a mercy from us.*
> *This is a matter already decreed."*
> *When she conceived him, she moved away,*
> *bearing him, to a faraway place.*
> **[Quran 19:16-22]**

The true date of birth for Jesus has always been in question, even among Christians. According to the Gospel of Luke, the angels announced the birth to shepherds who were tending their sheep on the hillsides at night. This indicates that the time of year could not have been bitter winter.

There is evidence in the Quran that Jesus was born late in September or early in October. This time of year is indicated because Mary *"shook the palm tree, and it dropped ripe dates for her."* Dates ripen in that part of the world during a very specific and narrow period, in late September and early October.

The Quran gives quite a bit of detail about the actual birth:
*The birth pangs came to her by the trunk of a palm tree.
She said, "(I am so ashamed),
I wish I were dead and completely forgotten."
(The baby) spoke to her: "Do not worry.
Your Lord has provided you with a stream of water
next to you, and shake the trunk of this palm tree;
it will drop ripe dates for you. Eat and drink and rejoice.
When you see anyone say, 'I have pledged to God
a pledge of silence; today, I shall not speak to anyone.' "
She carried him back to her family.
They said, "O Mary, you have committed a horrendous crime!
O descendant of Aaron, your father was not an evil man,
nor was your mother unchaste."
She simply pointed to the baby.
They said, "How can we communicate with
an infant in the cradle?"
The baby spoke and said, "I am a servant of God.
God has decreed that I shall receive the scripture;
He has appointed me a prophet.
He rendered me blessed wherever I might be.
He has exhorted me to observe the contact prayers
and the giving of alms, for as long as I live,
and to honor my mother.
He did not make me an evil tyrant.
Peace is my lot the day I was born, the day I die,*

and the day I am resurrected."
This is the true story of Jesus, son of Mary,
about whom they still conjecture.
It never befits God to have a son; be He glorified.
To have anything done, He simply says to it, "Be," and it is.
Jesus himself preached: "God is my Lord and your Lord;
you shall worship Him alone. For this is the right path."
[Quran 19:23-36]

It is apparent from this narration that the Bible's account of the virgin birth includes a number of different elements from those in the Quran. Given the Bible's need to explain Jesus' relation to the line of David, and what we have already seen to be indications of human interference in its text, we can be comfortable with the greater reliability of the Quran's account.

It is interesting that the Quranic elements of the date palm and water provided to Mary at the time of her labor are found in the Apocrypha, though when Jesus was an older child. The charges of fornication brought against Mary are also mentioned in the Apocrypha, in the description of Jesus' trial before Pilate. See *THE BIBLE OF THE WORLD,* edited by Robert O. Ballou, Viking Press, 1939, pp. 1258 & 1261.

The fact that Jesus spoke with wisdom even from the cradle is also in the Apocryphal book of *I. Infancy of Jesus Christ.* See *THE LOST BOOKS OF THE BIBLE,* Ibid., p. 38.

OTHER EXTRAORDINARY BIRTHS

The virgin birth of Jesus Christ was not the only extraordinary birth mentioned in the scriptures. Both the Bible and the Quran teach that Adam, Eve, Isaac, John the Baptist, and perhaps others have all come into being through uncommon or miraculous means.

Abraham and Sarah were very old when their son Isaac was conceived. Not only was Sarah old, far beyond menopause, she also had been sterile all of her life. The same was true with John the Baptist; his parents were much too old to have a child, and his mother was sterile. Thus, the creation of Isaac in the womb of Sarah, and the creation of John in the womb of Elizabeth were just as miraculous as the creation of Jesus inside Mary's womb.

> *But the Lord said to Abraham, "Why did Sarah laugh and say*
> *'Shall I really bear a child, old as I am?'*
> *Is anything too marvelous for the Lord to do?*
> *At the appointed time, about this time next year,*
> *I will return to you, and Sarah will have a son."*
> **[Genesis 18:13-14]**
> **[Quran 11:73]**

Zachariah was so impressed by the young girl Mary, for whom he was guardian, that he prayed for an equally pious child:

> *...Whenever Zachariah entered her sanctuary,*
> *he found provisions with her.*
> *He would ask, "Mary, where did you get this from?"*
> *She would say, "It is from God. God provides*
> *for whomever He chooses, without limits."*
> *That is when Zachariah implored his Lord:*
> *"My Lord, grant me such a good child;*
> *You are the Hearer of prayers."*
> **[Quran 3:37-38]**

> *(Zachariah and Elizabeth) were childless,*
> *for Elizabeth was sterile;*
> *moreover, both were advanced in years.*
> *...The angel said to him: "Do not be frightened,*
> *Zachariah; your prayer has been heard.*
> *Your wife Elizabeth shall bear a son*
> *whom you shall name John."*
> **[Luke 1:7,13]**

HOW IS VIRGIN BIRTH POSSIBLE?

How was Jesus born without a father? The Quran draws an analogy between the birth of Jesus and the creation of Adam. If God created

Adam without a father, or a mother, why should it be strange that He created a man from a mother and no father? The birth of Jesus without a father completes the picture of extraordinary creations:

1. the creation of a man, Adam, with neither a father nor a mother;
2. the creation of a woman, Eve, from a 'father' (Adam) and no mother; and finally,
3. the creation of a man, Jesus, from a mother and no father.

In the mathematically composed account of the Quran, it is significant that the assertion that *"the creation of Jesus is **equal** to the creation of Adam,"* is backed up by the fact that both Adam and Jesus are mentioned in the Quran exactly twenty-five times each. This reflects the numerical structuring of the Quran. Given all the other mathematical coding, this could not be a coincidence.

The creation of Jesus, as far as God is concerned,
*is **equal** to the creation of Adam;*
God created Adam from clay, then said to him,
"Be," and he was.
[Quran 3:59]

The key word here is 'Be.' Thus, God commanded that Jesus be formed inside the virgin Mary's womb, in much the same manner as He commanded that Adam be created, and Jesus was formed without a father. God simply said the word 'Be,' and he was. The divine command 'Be' is possibly 'The Word' or 'The Logos' that both the Bible and the Quran mention in connection with Jesus:

In the beginning was the Word;
the Word was in God's presence....
[John 1:1]

The angels said, "O Mary,
God sends good news to you;
a 'Word' from Him, to be named the Messiah,
Jesus the son of Mary.
Great will be his dignity in this world,
as well as in the Hereafter;

*he shall be one of those
who are close to Me."*
[Quran 3:45]

*O followers of the scriptures,
do not exceed the limits in practicing your religion,
and do not attribute to God other than the truth.
The Messiah, Jesus the son of Mary,
is a messenger of God and* **His Word***,
which He bestowed upon Mary;
a divine order from Him.
Therefore, you shall believe in God and His messengers,
and do not say, "Trinity."
You shall refrain (from such an utterance) for your own good.
God is only one God; be He glorified;
it is not befitting that God should beget a son.
To Him belongs everything in the heavens and the earth.
God suffices as protector.*
[Quran 4:171]

The Quran even gives us some details on the immaculate conception. It tells us that Jesus, like Adam, was created with the divine breath:

*Your Lord said to the angels,
"I am creating a human being from aged mud,
like the potter's clay.
Once I perfect him, and blow into him from My spirit,
you shall fall prostrate before him."*
[Quran 15:28-29]

*And (recall) the one who maintained her virginity,
then we blew into her from our spirit.
We rendered her and her son
a sign for the whole world.*
[Quran 21:91]

THE QUESTION OF JOSEPH

It is generally accepted by Christians that Mary was married to Joseph prior to the birth of Jesus. This understanding is derived from verses in the Gospels of Matthew and Luke:

> *Jacob was the father of Joseph the husband of Mary.*
> *It was of her that Jesus who is called the Messiah was born.*
> **[Matthew 1:16]**

> *Now this is how the birth of Jesus Christ came about.*
> *When his mother Mary was engaged to Joseph,*
> *but before they lived together,*
> *she was found with child through the power of the Holy Spirit.*
> *Joseph her husband, an upright man unwilling*
> *to expose her to the law, decided to divorce her quietly.*
> **[Matthew 1:18-19]**

> *And so Joseph went from the town of Nazareth*
> *in Galilee to Judea, to David's town of Bethlehem—*
> *because he was of the house and lineage of David—*
> *to register with Mary, his espoused wife, who was with child.*
> **[Luke 2:4-5]**

The concept of Mary's marriage to Joseph is peculiar indeed, coming from people who believe in the virgin birth of Christ. It brings into serious doubt the whole idea of virgin birth. In fact, Vincent Taylor theorizes: "It is also possible, and even probable, that the Matthean Genealogy ended originally with the words, 'And Joseph begat Jesus, who is called Christ' (Mt. i. 16)." [Ibid., p.10]

Interestingly, the Quran totally supports the idea of Jesus' virgin birth. The mathematically authenticated account in the Quran does not mention anything about Mary's marriage to anyone. There is no mention of Joseph.

The context of the Quranic narration conveys the clear message that Mary was neither married, nor unchaste, nor touched by any man prior to the birth of Jesus. Since Mary's marriage after the birth of Jesus is irrelevant to his birth, as well as to religious doctrine, the Quran does not mention whether Mary was ever married or not.

CONCLUSION

The virgin birth is reported in the Bible, the Apocrypha and the Quran. Though the details are somewhat different, in all cases Mary is held in great esteem, and her virgin pregnancy is recognized as a great honor.

The Quran's mathematical code stamps it as authentic, and the Quran itself gives us new insights into how such a miraculous birth could have taken place.

Chapter Twelve

JESUS' MIRACLES

> *In reply, Jesus said to them:*
> *"Go back and report to John what you hear and see:*
> *the blind recover their sight, cripples walk,*
> *lepers are cured, the deaf hear,*
> *dead men are raised to life,*
> *and the poor have the good news preached to them.*
> *Blest is the man who finds*
> *no stumbling block in me."*
> **[Matthew 11:4-6]**

Human beings have always been fascinated by the supernatural and by miracles. Often the desire to see miracles is stronger than the desire to know the truth.

Jesus encountered this, as is illustrated in Matthew 12:38. He was teaching, after being charged with using the help of Satan to expel the demon from a blind mute man when:

> *Some of the scribes and Pharisees then spoke up, saying,*
> *"Teacher, we want to see you work some signs."*
> **[Matthew 12:38]**

As if they had not just seen a sign!

WHAT IS A MIRACLE?

Living as we do in an age of modern technological miracles, we have perhaps become somewhat jaded. After all, modern medicine brings about miraculous cures for hitherto hopeless cases on a daily basis. Surgeons have even been known to revive the dead—when they lose someone on the operating table, and then are able to resuscitate them.

For us, many of the most astonishing miracles of Jesus are no longer that exceptional. In fact, many disregard them totally. That is why God sends signs or miracles which speak to the people of the time. For the contemporaries of Jesus, miraculous healings were appropriate signs. For modern times, an intricate code pervading the fabric of a 1400 year old scripture is more effective.

So what is a miracle?

Reginald Fuller begins with the following definition in his *"INTERPRETING THE MIRACLES"* (Westminster Press, 1963. pp. 8-9):

> A...scholarly definition, approved by many modern theologians, is that of St. Augustine: a miracle is an occurrence which is contrary to what is known of nature.

He then expands:

> Everything that happens in the realm of what we call nature is the handiwork of God himself....Nature merely furnishes the stage for the major work of God.... History is the arena where God intervenes specifically from time to time, succouring men, pressing his demands upon them and judging them for their disobedience. It is these extraordinary interventions which, properly speaking, are the miracles of the Bible. They are not necessarily breaches of the laws of nature.... But they are sufficiently startling, unusual and unexpected to call attention to themselves.

Thus, for Fuller the miracles of Jesus were the manifestations of God's action through him. This is a good definition for our purposes.

THE PURPOSE OF MIRACLES

The scriptures demonstrate that miracles serve two main purposes:

1. They serve as authenticating proofs that the messengers are indeed authorized by God to deliver His messages. When Moses, for example,

was dispatched to Egypt's Pharaoh and assigned the task of delivering the Children of Israel out of Egypt, he was given certain miracles to prove that he was carrying out divine orders. He threw down his staff, and it turned into a serpent before Pharaoh's eyes.

> *Then the Lord told Moses and Aaron,*
> *"If Pharaoh demands that you work*
> *a sign or wonder, you shall say to Aaron:*
> *Take your staff and throw it down before Pharaoh,*
> *and it will be changed into a snake."*
> **[Exodus 7:8-9]**

> *Moses said, "O Pharaoh, I am a messenger*
> *from the Lord of the universe.*
> *My assignment is to deliver to you God's truth.*
> *I come to you with a message from your Lord:*
> *Let the Children of Israel go."*
> *Pharaoh said, "If you brought a sign, let us see it,*
> *if you are truthful."*
> *Moses then threw down his staff,*
> *and it turned into a great serpent.*
> *He took out his hand, and it looked white to the beholders.*
> **[Quran 7:104-108]**

This type of miracle was Moses' sign that he was empowered by God to perform miracles and to deliver God's message to Pharaoh.

2. Miracles also can serve as a practical means of carrying out God's plan under extraordinary circumstances. A good example is Moses' parting of the Red Sea. The Children of Israel were being led by Moses out of Egypt, toward the holy land. Pharaoh and his army were in hot pursuit.

Suddenly, Moses and his people found themselves trapped between the Red Sea in front of them, and Pharaoh's army behind them. God inspired Moses to strike the sea with his staff, whereupon the sea split. Thus God carried out His plan of delivering the Israelites from the Egyptians' tyranny.

> *Then the Lord said to Moses,*
> *"Why are you crying out to Me? Tell the Israelites to go forward.*

*And you, lift up your staff and,
with hand outstretched over the sea,
split the sea in two, that the Israelites may
pass through it on dry land."*
                    [Exodus 14:15-16]

*The Egyptians pursued them towards the East.
When the two groups could see each other,
Moses' companions said, "We will get caught."
He said, "No way; my Lord is with me.
He will show me the way out."
We then inspired Moses: "Strike the sea with your staff."
Whereupon, the sea parted; each part like a great hill (of water).
Thus, we enabled them to pass through;
we delivered Moses and those who accompanied him,
and we drowned the others.*
                    [Quran 26:60-66]

JESUS' MIRACLES NOW PROVEN

The miracles manifested through Jesus were numerous and profound. All miracles, manifested through any of God's messengers, have been controversial. Many believers accept such extraordinary events on faith, others harbor doubts, and the majority of people do not believe in miracles at all—even when they have just seen one—like the accusers of Jesus who had just seen him expel a demon and then asked to see a sign!

However, as we have said before, we now have new evidence regarding the miracles narrated in the scripture. We now possess tangible, incontrovertible evidence confirming that such miracles did indeed take place. Thus, any numerically structured narration of an unusual event brings to us not only the event itself, but also a built-in proof that this event did take place.

THE MIRACLES THROUGH JESUS

While some of the miracles attributed to Jesus are mentioned in the

Bible, often with the same miracle described in more that one Gospel, a number of his miracles are unique to the Quran. Some of the latter are confirmed in apocryphal writings.

Many books have been written on the miracles of Jesus, with arguments for and against their validity. To my knowledge, none of them reference the Quran. Yet, we now have Quranic verification for a number of those miracles:

1. Jesus' virgin birth is of course the first miraculous phenomenon associated with Jesus. Of all of the descendants of Adam and Eve, Jesus is the only human being to be conceived without a father. For the scriptural references dealing with his birth, see the previous chapter.

2. Jesus spoke as a newborn infant. This miracle was mainly manifested to absolve his mother of an otherwise obvious violation of the extremely strict Mosaic law against sexual activity outside of marriage. Certainly, when a newborn infant speaks, and with great wisdom, the audience listens. Mary was thus absolved of any immorality. Had this not been the case, she would surely have been stoned to death, as required by Mosaic law.

This unique and convincing miracle of speaking as a newborn also established the identity of Jesus as the expected Messiah, and God's messenger to the Children of Israel.

While none of the canonized Gospels make any mention of this significant miracle, it is reported in Apocrypha as well as in the Quran:

*The following accounts we found in the book of Joseph
the high-priest, called by some Caiaphas:
He relates that Jesus spake even when he was in the cradle,
and said to his mother: "Mary, I am Jesus,
that word which thou didst bring forth
according to the declaration of the angel Gabriel to thee,
and my father has sent me for the salvation of the world."*
[LOST BOOKS OF THE BIBLE, I:1-3, p. 38]

*Mary returned to her family carrying the baby.
They said, "O Mary, you have committed a horrendous crime.*

*O descendant of Aaron, your father was
never an evil man, nor was your mother unchaste."
She simply pointed to the baby;
they gasped, "How can we communicate
with an infant in the cradle?"
(The infant Jesus) spoke and said, "I am a servant of God.
He has decreed that I shall receive the scripture;
He has appointed me a prophet."*
[Quran 19:27-30]

3. Jesus shaped birds from clay, then blew into them, and they became live birds *"by God's leave."* Again, the canonized Gospels do not mention this 'creation' miracle. However, this miracle is described in the Apocrypha, and the Quran mentions it prominently in two places, 3:49 and 5:110. The Quran makes it clear that Jesus' blowing into the clay figures was done *"by God's leave"* and that it parallels God's blowing into the clay figure of Adam to give him life:

*Your Lord said to the angels,
"I am creating a human being from aged potters' clay.
Once I perfect him and blow into him from My spirit,
you shall bow down before him."*
[Quran 15:28-29]

*God taught Jesus the scripture and wisdom:
the Torah and the Gospel.
He sent him as a messenger to the Children of Israel,
saying,"I come to you with a sign from your Lord:
I create for you from clay, the figures of birds,
then I blow into them, and they become live birds by God's leave."*
[Quran 3:48-49]

*Then Jesus took from the bank of the stream
some soft clay and formed out of it twelve sparrows....
Then Jesus, clapping together the palms of his hands,
called to the sparrows, and said to them:
Go, fly away; and while ye live remember me.
So the sparrows fled away, making a noise.*

*The Jews seeing this, were astonished, and went away,
and told their chief persons what a strange miracle
they had seen wrought by Jesus.*
[LOST BOOKS OF THE BIBLE, pp. 60-61]

4. As mentioned earlier in this chapter, miraculous healings were important signs for Jesus' contemporaries. In fact, if you categorize all the miracles of Jesus given in the Gospels, healings and the expelling of disabling demons count as the vast majority. Jesus cured a number of different ailments by God's leave.

In Matthew 9:1-8, we see that he healed a man who was paralyzed:

*...[Jesus] then said to the paralyzed man—
"Stand up! Roll up your mat, and go home."
The man stood up and went toward his home.
At the sight, a feeling of awe came over the crowd,
and they praised God for giving such authority to men.*
[Matthew 9:6-8]

Leprosy, a dreaded and incurable disease, was miraculously treated. Lepers were restored to health by Jesus:

*A leper approached him with a request,
kneeling down as he addressed him:
"If you will to do so, you can cure me."
Moved with pity, Jesus stretched out his hand,
touched him, and said: "I will do it. Be cured."
The leprosy left then and there, and he was cured.*
[Mark 1:40-42]

A man with a shriveled hand was cured, as reported in Matthew:

*[Jesus] left that place and went into their synagogue.
A man with a shriveled hand happened to be there,
and they put this question to Jesus,
hoping to bring an accusation against him:
"Is it lawful to work a cure on the sabbath?"
He said in response: "Suppose one of you has a sheep*

> and it falls into a pit on the sabbath.
> Will he not take hold of it and pull it out?
> Well, think how much more precious
> a human being is than a sheep.
> Clearly, good deeds may be performed on the sabbath."
> To the man he said, "Stretch out your hand."
> He did so, and it was perfectly restored;
> it became as sound as the other.
> **[Matthew 12:9-13]**

The cure of a woman who was hemorrhaging is reported in Luke:

> A woman with a hemorrhage of twelve years duration,
> incurable at any doctor's hands,
> came up behind him
> and touched the tassel on his cloak.
> Immediately her bleeding stopped.
> Jesus asked, "Who touched me?"
> Everyone disclaimed doing it, while Peter said,
> "Lord, the crowds are milling and pressing around you!"
> Jesus insisted, "Someone touched me;
> I know that power has gone forth from me."
> **[Luke 8:43-46]**

There are reports of additional healing incidents. One is where Jesus cured a nobleman's son:

> ...At Capernaum there happened to be a royal official
> whose son was ill.
> When he heard that Jesus had come back from Judea to
> Galilee, he went to him and begged him
> to come down and restore health to his son, who was near death.
> Jesus replied, "Unless you people see signs and
> wonders, you do not believe."
> "Sir," the royal official pleaded with him,
> "come down before my child dies."
> Jesus told him, "Return home. Your son will live..."
> He was on his way home
> when his servants met him

with the news that his boy was going to live....
He and his whole household
thereupon became believers.
[John 4:46-53]

Peter's mother-in-law was healed by Jesus when she suffered from fever:

Simon's mother-in-law lay ill with a fever,
and the first thing they did was to tell him about her.
He went over to her and grasped her hand
and helped her up, and the fever left her.
She immediately began to wait on them.
[Mark 1:30-31]

While the Quran does not validate these specific incidents of healing, Jesus' ability to heal, *"by God's leave,"* is documented there. In Chapter 3, Mary is addressed by the angel sent to deliver to her the news of a son:

"As a messenger to the Children of Israel, he will proclaim:
'I come to you with proof from your Lord....
I restore vision to the blind, I heal the leprous,
and I revive the dead by God's leave....'"
[Quran 3:49]

In the Quran's Chapter 5, Verse 110 God Himself addresses Jesus on the Day of Resurrection:

"...You healed the blind and the leprous by My leave,
and revived the dead by My leave...."
[Quran 5:110]

5. The last two verses quoted directly above tell us that Jesus also restored sight to the hopelessly blind. This is also reported in the Gospel of Matthew:

As Jesus moved on from there,
two blind men came after him crying out,
"Son of David, have pity on us!"
When he got to the house,
the blind men caught up with him.

> Jesus said to them, "Are you confident I can do this?"
> "Yes, Lord," they told him.
> At that he touched their eyes and said,
> "Because of your faith it shall be done to you;"
> and they recovered their sight...
> **[Matthew 9:27-30]**

6. The Gospels and the Quran report a number of incidents where Jesus restored life, *"by God's leave,"* to a number of different people who had died:

> Soon afterward he went to a town called Naim,
> and his disciples and a large crowd accompanied him.
> As he approached the gate of the town
> a dead man was being carried out,
> the only son of a widowed mother.
> A considerable crowd of townsfolk were with her.
> Jesus was moved with pity upon seeing her
> and said to her, "Do not cry."
> Then he stepped forward and touched the litter;
> at this, the bearers halted.
> He said, "Young man, I bid you get up."
> The dead man sat up and began to speak.
> Then Jesus gave him back to his mother.
> Fear seized them all and they began to praise God.
> "A great prophet has risen among us," they said....
> **[Luke 7:11-16]**

> Before Jesus had finished speaking to them,
> a synagogue leader came up, did him reverence,
> and said, "My daughter has just died. Please come
> and lay your hand on her and she will come back to life."
> Jesus stood up and followed him, and his disciples did the same...
> When Jesus arrived at the synagogue leader's house
> and saw the flute players and the crowd
> who were making a din, he said, "Leave, all of you!
> The little girl is not dead. She is asleep."

At this they began to ridicule him.
When the crowd had been put out
he entered and took her by the hand, and the little girl got up.
[Matthew 9:18-19, 23-25]

God says to Jesus, the son of Mary, (on the Day of Resurrection),
"I have bestowed many a favor upon you and your mother;
I supported you with the Holy Spirit
which enabled you to speak as a newborn infant,
as well as when you grew up;
I taught you the scripture, wisdom, the Torah, and the Gospel;
you created from clay the figures of birds, by My leave;
you healed the hopelessly blind and the lepers, by My leave;
and you revived the dead, by My leave.
I protected you from the Children of Israel
when you went to them with these clear signs
and wonders; those among them who disbelieved said,
'This is no more than witchcraft.'"
[Quran 5:110]

The best known incident where Jesus revived the dead, the resurrection of Lazarus, is reported in the Gospel of John:

...Jesus looked upward and said:
"Father, I thank you for having heard me.
I know that you always hear me but
I have said this for the sake of the crowd,
that they may believe that you sent me."
Having said this, he called loudly, "Lazarus, come out!"
The dead man came out, bound hand and foot
with linen strips, his face wrapped in cloth.
"Untie him," Jesus told them, "and let him go free."
[John 11:41-44]

7. One of Jesus' miracles which is clearly stated in the Quran and in the Gospel of John is that he exhibited extrasensory abilities:

(Jesus said,) "...I can tell you what you ate
and what you store in your homes.

> *These should be sufficient signs for you*
> *if you are believers."*
> **[Quran 3:49]**

He also showed these abilities when talking with the Samarian woman at Jacob's well:

> *He said to her, "Go call your husband,*
> *and then come back here."*
> *"I have no husband," replied the woman.*
> *"You are right in saying you have no husband!"*
> *Jesus exclaimed. "The fact is, you have had five,*
> *and the man you are living with now is not your husband.*
> *What you said is true."*
> *"Sir," answered the woman, "I can see you are a prophet."*
> **[John 4:16-19]**

8. According to the Quran, Jesus' disciples challenged him to bring down a feast from the sky. After some hesitation, he prayed for such a feast. God answered Jesus' prayer and a feast descended for Jesus and his disciples:

> *The disciples said, "O Jesus, son of Mary,*
> *Could your Lord send down to us a feast from the sky?"*
> *He said, "Reverence God, if you are really believers."*
> *They said, "We wish to eat therefrom,*
> *and to assure our hearts, and to know*
> *that you have told us the truth. We wish to be witnesses thereof."*
> *Jesus, son of Mary, said, "Our God and our Lord,*
> *send down to us a feast from the sky.*
> *Let it satisfy each and every one of us;*
> *a provision from you. You are the best provider."*
> *God said, "I am sending it down.*
> *But then, if any of you disbelieves thereafter,*
> *I will surely commit him to such retribution*
> *as I never imposed on anyone else."*
> **[Quran 5:112-115]**

The closest thing to this miracle in the Gospels are the reports of Jesus feeding the multitudes, as in Matthew 14:15-21 where Jesus was reported to have fed five thousand.

All of these miracles make it very clear that Jesus was God's messenger and special servant. In fact, the Quran recognizes that Jesus was given a special honor. It tells us that Jesus was *"born as a prophet of God."* This is amply demonstrated by the proven fact that Jesus preached the worship of God alone from the time he was a newborn infant.

This prophethood from birth is reflected in the fact that the Quran reports errors committed by many other prophets and/or messengers of God, including Moses, Abraham, Muhammad and all of the best known prophets, but no mistakes are attributed to Jesus.

CONCLUSION
While the Quran stresses the humanity of Jesus, it also honors him as a prophet from birth. In its mathematically guarded verses, it relates many miracles which God performed through him. In doing so, it confirms the validity of those miracles.

For the first time in human history we know for a fact that indeed Jesus did raise the dead, heal the hopelessly blind and the afflicted.

We also know that these, and his other miracles do not in any way confer divinity upon him.

Chapter Thirteen

JESUS' DEATH

*It was now around midday,
and darkness came over the whole land
until midafternoon with an eclipse of the sun.
The curtain in the sanctuary was torn in two.
Jesus uttered a loud cry and said, "Father,
into your hands I commend my spirit."
After he said this, he expired.
The centurion, upon seeing what
had happened, gave glory to God by saying,
"Surely this was an innocent man."*
[Luke 23:44-47]

Almost all Christians believe that Jesus was tortured and then crucified to death. Still, there is a great deal of conjecture and speculation about the last days of Jesus. As mentioned before, some rather radical theories exist regarding the crucifixion, including that someone else was crucified instead, or that Jesus did not die but was in a coma when removed from the cross.

There are no reports of the event from neutral or even hostile sources. For Christians the only source of information on this extremely important event has been the Bible. Even the Gospels are full of contradictions regarding this event.

MATTHEW & MARK
The Gospel of Matthew gives the following account:
> The procurator's soldiers took Jesus inside the praetorium
> and collected the whole cohort around him.
> They stripped off his clothes and
> wrapped him in a scarlet military cloak.
> Weaving a crown of thorns they fixed it on his head,
> and stuck a reed in his right hand.
> Then they began to mock him by dropping to their knees
> before him, saying, "All hail, king of the Jews!"
> They also spat at him. Afterward they took hold
> of the reed and kept striking him on the head.
> Finally, when they had finished making a fool of him,
> they stripped him of the cloak, dressed him in his own clothes,
> and led him off to crucifixion. On their way out,
> they met a Cyrenian named Simon.
> This man they pressed into service to carry the cross.
> Upon arriving at a site called Golgotha
> (a name which means Skull Place), they gave him
> a drink of wine flavored with gall,
> which he tasted but refused to drink.
> When they had crucified him, they divided his
> clothes among them by casting lots;
> then they sat down there and kept watch over him.
> Above his head they put the charge against him in writing:
> "THIS IS JESUS, KING OF THE JEWS."
> Two insurgents were crucified along with him,
> one at his right and one at his left.
> People going by kept insulting him,
> tossing their heads and saying:
> "So you are the one who was going to destroy the temple
> and rebuild it in three days! Save yourself, why don't you?
> Come down off that cross if you are God's Son!"
> The chief priests, the scribes, and the elders,
> also joined in the jeering:
> "He saved others but he cannot save himself!

So he is the king of Israel!
Let's see him come down from that cross and
then we will believe in him.
He relied on God; let God rescue him now if he wants to.
After all, he claimed, 'I am God's Son.' "
The insurgents who had been crucified with him
kept taunting him in the same way.
From noon onward there was darkness
over the whole land until midafternoon.
Then toward midafternoon Jesus cried out
in a loud tone, "Eli, Eli, lema sabachthani?"
that is, "My God, my God, why have you forsaken me?"
[Matthew 27:27-46]

While the Gospel of John, like Matthew above, narrates that the procurator's soldiers were the ones who took Jesus inside to torture him and crucify him, the Gospel of Mark states that *"the chief priests, with the elders and scribes (that is, the whole Sanhedren) bound Jesus, led him away, and handed him over to Pilate."* Generally, however, Mark's account is similar to that given in Matthew's Gospel.

LUKE

Luke's narration of Jesus' death is significantly different from that of Matthew and Mark. According to Luke, Jesus was sent by Pilate to Herod, then back to Pilate, then he narrates that Jesus delivered a short sermon on route to his crucifixion:

As they led him away, they laid hold of one Simon the Cyrenean
who was coming in from the fields.
They put a crossbeam on Simon's shoulder for
him to carry along behind Jesus.
A great crowd of people followed him,
including women who beat their breasts and
lamented over him. Jesus turned to them and said:
"Daughters of Jerusalem, do not weep for me.
Weep for yourselves and for your children.
The days are coming when they will say,

*'Happy are the sterile, the wombs that never
bore and the breasts that never nursed.'
Then they will begin saying to the mountains,
'Fall on us,' and to the hills, 'Cover us.'
If they do these things in the green wood,
what will happen in the dry?"
Two others who were criminals were led along with him
to be crucified. When they came to Skull Place,
as it was called, they crucified him there
and the criminals as well, one on his right and
the other on his left.
[Jesus said, "Father, forgive them;
they do not know what they are doing."]*
[Luke 23:26-34]

JOHN'S ACCOUNT
*Jesus was led away, and carrying the cross by himself,
went out to what is called the Place of the Skull
(In Hebrew, Golgotha). There they crucified him,
and two others with him: one on either side,
Jesus in the middle. Pilate had an inscription placed
on the cross which read,
JESUS THE NAZOREAN
THE KING OF THE JEWS.*
[John 19:16-19]

John's report of the events immediately preceding the crucifixion has Jesus carrying the cross himself. The inscription on the cross is quite different here from that in the other Gospels.

There are many other discrepancies among the narrations of Jesus' death. From the Bible alone it is impossible to know what really happened at that time.

Some of these discrepancies can be understood by the fact that Jesus' contemporaries had different understandings of his death. Willi

Marxsen clearly points this out (see *JESUS AND EASTER*, Abingdon Press, 1990. pp. 54-55):

> It cannot be disputed that different circles in early Christianity held to different understandings of the death of Jesus. In the material of the Synoptic tradition there is the thought that the death of Jesus was a consequence of his activity. Jesus is portrayed there as one who by his activities risked persecution, and even death. He is not, however, portrayed as one who had wanted his own death, or even as one who had understood it as a vicarious or atoning death. The idea of the death of Jesus as an "atonement" is foreign to the material of the Synoptic tradition (although it was later inserted at two places, Mark 10:45 and 14:24). Rather, Jesus dies because he hazarded death in the way he carried on his activity.
>
> In the formulas and especially in Paul's letters, the understanding of Jesus' death as an atonement is evident. Historically and theologically this idea has been of greater significance, yet it is only one understanding of the death of Jesus.

The fact remains that from the Bible alone we can not get a clear picture of what actually happened.

QURAN'S MATHEMATICALLY CODED ACCOUNT

Fortunately, with the discovery of mathematically authenticated scripture, we have a reliable reference that enables us to sift through the various narrations of this event.

The account of Jesus' death in the Quran is startling. It states: *"they never killed Jesus; they never crucified him; they were only made to think that they did."* :

> *They claimed that they killed the Messiah,*
> *Jesus, the son of Mary, the messenger of God.*
> *In fact, they never killed him;*
> *they never crucified him;*
> *they were only made to think that they did.*
> *Indeed, those who speculate about him*
> *are full of doubt about their own accounts;*
> *they are never sure.*

They only conjecture. What is absolutely certain is:
they never killed him. Instead, God raised him to Him.
God is Almighty, Most Wise.
[Quran 4:157-158]

Undoubtedly, this Quranic narration represents a new and profound account of the death of Jesus. It is bound to shock most people, so some explanation is in order.

The Quran consistently talks about the 'real person,' i.e., the soul, when talking about anyone. The Quran differentiates between two human entities: a temporary entity, the body, and an eternal entity which is 'the person.' The temporary entity is considered a shell or a garment worn by the lasting entity. The Quran does not regard this temporary shell as 'the person.'

The importance of the body, or the person's outer shell, is in serving the real person by effecting sufficient growth and development of the soul in preparation for the real, eternal life (of the Hereafter). If we look upon one's body as a wild horse, one attains the required growth and development by taming and controlling the whims of this horse. At the end of one's predetermined interim in this life, one sheds the shell and moves on towards the eternal Hereafter; the body's role ends.

Thus, when the Quran states that *"they never crucified Jesus; they never killed him,"* the word *"him"* here refers to the real Jesus, not his body.

The body may be present somewhere, but the person may or may not be present with it. People who are familiar with 'out-of-body experiences' know that the body is nothing more than a garment or a physical vehicle for the soul. In out-of-body experiences, the intellect remains with the person, not with the body. Those who practice out-of-body (or astral projection) experiments often describe the body as just laying there like an inanimate object.

The Quran explains clearly that Jesus, the real person, was 'raised to God' prior to any torture or crucifixion. Those who believed that they were torturing or crucifying Jesus were in fact dealing with Jesus' body, an empty shell devoid of feelings and knowledge.

Being 'raised to God' indicates another important fact—that the righteous go directly to heaven, and do not wait for the Day of Resurrection to attain Paradise:

> THE RIGHTEOUS DO NOT DIE; when their lives on this earth come to the predetermined end, the angel of death simply invites them to leave their earthly bodies and move on to Heaven, the same Paradise where Adam and Eve once lived. Heaven has been in existence since Adam and Eve. We learn from 89:27-30 that God invites the believers' souls: "Enter My Paradise."

The above quote is from an article written by Dr. Rashad Khalifa, the discoverer of the Quran's mathematical code (*SUBMITTERS PERSPECTIVE*, Masjid Tucson, Feb., 1990). He continues:

> As far as people on earth are concerned, the righteous "die." People do not realize that the righteous simply leave their bodies, and move on to Paradise....The righteous go to Paradise, while their friends and relatives are still living on earth. Like going to Hawaii and waiting for us there.

He cites several verses which are well worth examining:

> *Give good news to those who believe and*
> *work righteousness that they will have gardens with flowing streams.*
> *When provided with provisions of fruits therein,*
> *they will say, "This is what was given to us in the past."*
> *They will be given similar provisions,*
> *and they will have pure spouses therein.*
> *They abide therein forever.*
> **[Quran 2:25]**

The indication in this verse is that the righteous are in a place similar to gardens of the Hereafter, with similar provisions. This would certainly be the case if they had been waiting in the Garden of Eden (also called Paradise), until the Day of Resurrection. Coupled with the following verses, that is the clear conclusion:

> *Do not think that those who are*
> *killed in the cause of God are dead;*
> *they are alive at their Lord, being provided for.*
> **[Quran 3:169]**

*Do not say about those who are killed in the cause of God,
"They are dead."
For they are alive, but you do not perceive.*
[Quran 2:154]

*(At the time of his death) he was told, "Enter Paradise."
He said, "I wish my people (on earth) knew
that my Lord has forgiven me and honored me."*
[Quran 36:26-27]

In the case of Jesus, all these mathematically coded verses show that God raised the real person, Jesus' soul, leaving his body for the torturers and crucifiers. Thus, they never tortured Jesus. They never crucified him. He was gone long before any torture or crucifixion of his body:

*They plotted and schemed, but so did God;
God is the best schemer.
Thus, God said, "O Jesus, I am putting you to death;
raising you to Me, and ridding you of the disbelievers.
I will make those who follow you high above
those who disbelieve until the Day of Resurrection.
Then to Me is the ultimate destiny of all of you.
Then I will judge among you concerning your disputes."*
[Quran 3:54-55]

It is astonishing to find this phenomenon, the separation of the real person from the still living body, indicated in the New Testament, and even more specifically stated in some apocryphal literature. There is an especially straightforward reference to this phenomenon reported by James Brashler in *THE NAG HAMMADI LIBRARY* (Harper & Row, 1977).

The Nag Hammadi Library is a collection of ancient documents unearthed at Nag Hammadi, Egypt. They are described as containing "the sacred scriptures of the Gnostic movement that emerged and rapidly grew in the cradle of civilization at the time of Jesus and early Christianity. Its codices are a priceless periscope into the tumultuous world of ideas brewing during one of civilization's great turning points."

158   JESUS: MYTHS & MESSAGE

James Brashler describes a vision seen by the apostle Peter, in his introduction to the Gnostic *Apocalypse of Peter* (Ibid., p. 339):

> The first visionary scene, is depicting the hostile priests and people about to kill Jesus (72,4-9)....The second scene (81,3-14) describes Peter's vision of the crucifixion of Jesus. The accompanying interpretation by Jesus makes a distinction between the external physical form and the living Jesus; the latter stands nearby laughing at his ignorant persecutors.

A clear distinction is thus made in this ancient literature, very close to the time of Jesus, between "the external physical form," i.e., the body of Jesus, and "the living Jesus." According to this narration, the real person of Jesus was unphased by the torturers and persecutors of his soulless body.

Looking at the translation of the *Apocalypse of Peter* itself (Ibid., p. 344), we find the startling vision of Peter:

> *When he had said those things,*
> *I saw him seemingly being seized by them.*
> *And I said, "What do I see, O Lord, that it is you yourself*
> *whom they take, and that you are grasping me?*
> *Or who is this one, glad and laughing, on the tree?*
> *And is it another one whose feet and hands they are striking?"*
> *The Savior said to me, "He whom you saw on the tree,*
> *glad and laughing, this is the living Jesus.*
> *But this one into whose hands and feet they drive the nails*
> *is the fleshy part."*
>   **[Apocalypse of Peter, VII, 3, 81]**

A careful examination of the Gospels of Mark and Luke reveals that Jesus was in fact gone prior to crucifixion. He did not respond to the surrounding chaos. This confirms the apocryphal account reported in the Nag Hammadi Library, and agrees with the mathematically authenticated account of the Quran:

> *The chief priests, meanwhile,*
> *brought many accusations against Jesus.*

Pilate interrogated him again:
"Surely you have some answer?
See how many accusations
they are leveling against you."
But greatly to Pilate's surprise,
Jesus made no further response.
[Mark 15:3-5]

Herod was extremely pleased to see Jesus.
From the reports about him he had wanted to see him,
and he was hoping to see him work some miracle.
He questioned Jesus at considerable length,
but Jesus made no answer.
The chief priests and scribes were at hand
to accuse him vehemently.
Herod and his guards then treated
him with contempt and insult....
[Luke 23:8-11]

Putting all these accounts together, this possible picture emerges:

1. The human being consists of two main distinct entities:

   a. the body, which serves as a mere shell or garment, and

   b. the soul, which is the real person.

2. In accordance with a predetermined plan, the time came for Jesus to complete his mission as God's messenger to the Children of Israel and as the Messiah. This coincided with the scheme of Jesus' adversaries to crucify him. Just before executing their plot, God's plan was implemented, and Jesus the real person was summoned or "raised to God."

3. Jesus' body was left for his persecutors to torture and crucify; they were dealing with an empty shell devoid of all feelings or understanding.

4. Thus, the Quran's mathematically coded statements that *"they never killed Jesus, they never crucified him; they were led to believe that they did,"* are accurate and proven facts.

MODERN DEMONSTRATION

Rashad Khalifa draws an interesting parallel between what he understands to be the case in Jesus' death, and that of a modern patient who underwent an historical surgical procedure. (See Khalifa's *QURAN THE FINAL TESTAMENT*, Ibid. Appendix 22, p. 667)

On November 25, 1984, William J. Schroeder, from Jasper, Indiana, received an artificial heart at Humana Heart Institute International of Louisville, Kentucky. The *NEW YORK TIMES* of Monday, November 26, 1984 published the following news item:

> SURGEONS IMPLANT MECHANICAL PUMP TO REPLACE HEART
> LOUISVILLE, KY, Nov 25 -- A 17-member surgical team today removed the diseased heart of a 52-year old man and replaced it with a plastic and metal pump....Dr. Devries leaned over Mr. Schroeder and said, "Everything went well, perfectly."

On Wednesday, December 12, 1984, the 18th day after receiving the artificial heart, Mr. Schroeder was so normal and so alert that when President Reagan talked with him he complained about a delay in sending his Social Security disability check. On the *nineteenth* day, December 13, 1984, the world was told that Mr. Schroeder "suffered a stroke."

What really happened was that Mr. Schroeder, the real person, departed. William J. Schroeder died. His body, the empty shell, continued to function through artificial means. The artificial heart continued to pump, and all other life processes of Mr. Schroeder's body continued to work. Significantly, from that moment on, he never recognized the date, the day or time. The *WASHINGTON POST* of Friday, December 14, 1984 published the following news:

> LOUISVILLE, Dec. 13---William J. Schroeder, who became the world's second recipient of an artificial heart 18 days ago, tonight suffered a stroke in his hospital bed as he ate dinner with his wife, doctors reported.... (Dr. A. M.) Lansing replied, "unequivocally, no," when asked if the stroke could have been a result of Schroeder's many activities recently. These included a telephone conversation with President Reagan Wednesday and fast government action earlier

Jesus' Death 161

today to deliver a Social Security disability check that he had told Reagan was overdue.

At Humana Hospital - Audubon, where the implant took place, Lansing said Schroeder was talking to his wife when "she noticed suddenly he stopped feeding himself and was just holding his food in his right hand." He appeared "drowsy, his eyes rolled back, and he became somewhat limp," Lansing said.

The stroke was not "life threatening," Lansing said. Shortly afterward, Schroeder was somewhat "stuporous" and "not talking intelligently," Lansing said.

In retrospect, it is obvious that William J. Schroeder actually left his body on the nineteenth day (December 13, 1984) after receiving the artificial heart on November 25, 1984. Schroeder was raised to God about 600 days—19 months—before his body finally ceased to function.

According to the Quran, this is precisely what happened to Jesus: he was raised to God before the crucifixion of his empty body:

They claimed that they killed the Messiah,
Jesus, the son of Mary, the messenger of God.
In fact, they never killed him; they never crucified him;
they were led to believe that they did....
For sure, they never killed him.
Instead, God raised him to Him.
God is Almighty, Most Wise.
[Quran 4:157-158]

Chapter Fourteen

JESUS' RESURRECTION

The resurrection narratives in the gospels do not derive directly from the primitive stage when the apostolic testimony was as yet unchallenged by the unbeliever. They reflect a somewhat later period, when the average Christian was aware of the unbeliever's principal counter-arguments against the doctrine of resurrection; namely, that Jesus' disciples had removed his body from the tomb, or that they were victims of visionary or other objectively unreal experiences. The gospels and the tradition that preceded them carefully interwove the data of the resurrection with the replies to these arguments, so that Christians might remain in peaceful possession of their faith.
 [NEW AMERICAN BIBLE - Footnote to Luke 24:1-53]

The above quoted footnote to Luke 24 makes it clear that the translators, who were intimately acquainted with the most ancient sources still extant, were aware that the various versions of the resurrection are contradictory. They were also aware that the versions accepted as integral portions of the New Testament were written at a later time than the rest of the narratives.

This is especially important to remember given that there were no eye witnesses to the resurrection itself. This means that the development of the resurrection narratives had no firm factual basis. They were statements of faith, rather than fact. (See W. Marxsen, *JESUS & EASTER*, Ibid., for an expansion of these arguments.)

Jesus' Resurrection

The reference to Jesus' resurrection in the Gospels is solely connected with a resurrection here in this life, three days after Jesus' crucifixion. However, a careful study of this subject unveils a tremendous amount of confusion, conjecture, and contradiction.

MATTHEW'S ACCOUNT

According to Matthew, *"Mary Magdalene and the other Mary"* came to the tomb to inspect it. As they waited there, an angel appeared and rolled away the stone which was blocking the entrance to the tomb. The angel spoke to the women telling them that Jesus had been resurrected. As they hurried away, *"half-overjoyed, half-fearful,"* Jesus appeared to them and told them to tell the disciples to go to Galilee where they would see him.

Matthew then goes into some detail about the reaction of the Romans to the resurrection, but says nothing about how the disciples received the news. Here are some of the last lines in the Gospel of Matthew:

When evening fell, a wealthy man from
Arimathea arrived, Joseph by name.
He was another of Jesus' disciples,
and had gone to request the body of Jesus.
Thereupon Pilate issued an order for its release.
Taking the body, Joseph wrapped it
in fresh linen and laid it in his own new tomb
which had been hewn from a formation of rock.
Then he rolled a huge stone across the entrance
of the tomb and went away.
But Mary Magdalene and the other Mary
remained sitting there, facing the tomb.
The next day, following the Day of Preparation,
the chief priests and the Pharisees
called at Pilate's residence. "Sir," they said,
"we have recalled that that imposter while he was
still alive made the claim, 'After three days I will rise.'
You should issue an order having the tomb
kept under surveillance until the third day.

*Otherwise his disciples may go and steal him and tell the people,
 'He has been raised from the dead!'
This final imposture would be worse than the first."
Pilate told them, "You have a guard. Go and
secure the tomb as best you can."
So they went and kept it under surveillance of the guard,
after fixing a seal to the stone.
After the sabbath, as the first day of the week was dawning,
Mary Magdalene came with the other Mary
to inspect the tomb. Suddenly there was a mighty earthquake,
as the angel of the Lord descended from heaven.
He came to the stone, rolled it back, and sat on it.
In appearance he resembled a flash of lightning
 while his garments were as dazzling as snow.
The guards grew paralyzed with fear of him and fell down
like dead men. Then the angel spoke,
addressing the women: "Do not be frightened.
I know you are looking for Jesus the crucified, but he is not here.
He has been raised, exactly as he promised.
Come and see the place where he was laid.
Then go quickly and tell his disciples:
'He has been raised from the dead and now goes ahead of you
to Galilee, where you will see him.'
That is the message I have for you."
They hurried away from the tomb half-overjoyed,
half-fearful, and ran to carry the good news to his disciples.
Suddenly, without warning,
Jesus stood before them and said, "Peace!"
The women came up and embraced his feet and did him homage.
At this Jesus said to them, "Do not be afraid!
Go and carry the news to my brothers
that they are to go to Galilee, where they will see me."
As the women were returning, some of the guard
went into the city and reported to the chief priests all that
had happened. They, in turn, convened with the elders
and worked out their strategy, giving the soldiers*

*a large bribe with the instructions: "You are to say,
'His disciples came during the night and stole him
while we were asleep.'
If any word of this gets to the procurator, we will straighten it out
with him and keep you out of trouble."
The soldiers pocketed the money and did
as they had been instructed.
This is the story that circulates among the Jews to this very day.*
[Matthew 27:57-28:15]

ACCORDING TO MARK
The Gospel of Mark relates that three women, the two Marys and Salome, went to the tomb just after sunrise. The stone blocking the tomb's entrance had already been rolled away and when they entered the tomb they found a young man dressed in white. He told them that Jesus had been resurrected and was going ahead to Galilee where they would see him. Frightened, they said nothing to anyone.

Mark ends abruptly there. The *NEW AMERICAN BIBLE* then gives us two different endings which may finish the story; one is found in the Marcan gospel and the other in some Greek manuscripts. Neither seems to fit comfortably into the flow of Mark's narration, nor do they agree with one another.

LUKE
Luke indicates that several women went to the tomb. The rock had been rolled back. While they were wondering over the disappearance of Jesus' body, *"two men in dazzling garments stood beside them."* The men told them that Jesus had been resurrected. The women went back and told the others, but were not believed. Peter also went to check. Jesus then appeared to two of his followers on the road to Emmaus. They did not recognize him until they sat to eat together, whereupon he vanished. When they returned to Jerusalem to tell the disciples, Jesus appeared among them all. They thought that he was a ghost and were frightened. He reassured them and spoke of his fulfillment of the ancient

prophecies. Then he led them out near Bethany, blessed them and ascended into heaven.

> *On the first day of the week, at dawn, the women*
> *came to the tomb bringing the spices they had prepared.*
> *They found the stone rolled back from the tomb;*
> *but when they entered the tomb,*
> *they did not find the body of the Lord Jesus.*
> *While they were still at a loss over what to think of this,*
> *two men in dazzling garments stood beside them.*
> *Terrified, the women bowed to the ground.*
> *The men said to them, "Why do you search*
> *for the Living One among the dead?*
> *He is not here; he has been raised up.*
> *Remember what he said to you while he was still in Galilee—*
> *that the Son of Man must be delivered into the hands*
> *of the sinful men, and be crucified, and on the third day rise again."*
> *With this reminder, his words came back to them.*
> *On their return from the tomb, they told all these things*
> *to the Eleven and the others.*
> *The women were Mary of Magdala, Joanna,*
> *and Mary the mother of James.*
> *The other women with them also told the apostles,*
> *but the story seemed like nonsense and they refused to believe them.*
> *Peter, however, got up and ran to the tomb.*
> *He stooped down but could see nothing but the wrappings.*
> *So he went away full of amazement at what had occurred.*
> **[Luke 24:1-12]**

JOHN'S ACCOUNT

According to the Gospel of John, Mary Magdalene went to the tomb by herself early in the morning while it was still dark. Seeing that the stone had been moved, she went back and found Simon Peter and the other disciple (described here in the Bible simply as the one Jesus loved but later defined as John himself). She told them: *"The Lord has been taken from the tomb! We don't know where they have put him!"*

These three returned to the tomb and Simon Peter actually entered, followed by John. Finding the tomb empty, the two disciples went home leaving Mary still there. While she wept, she saw two angels and then Jesus.

She thought he was the gardener until he called her by her name. He told her, *"go to my brothers and tell them, 'I am ascending to my Father and your Father, to my God and your God!'"* She did so.

That evening Jesus appeared to his disciples (with the exception of Thomas, who was missing). He entered, even though the doors where they were meeting in secrecy were locked. He said to them: *"As the Father has sent me, so I send you....Receive the Holy Spirit. If you forgive men's sins, they are forgiven them; if you hold them bound, they are held bound."*

A week later he appeared to them again. This time Thomas was also present and was convinced of his resurrection.

John then states that Jesus performed other signs not included in the gospel: *"But these have been recorded to help you believe that Jesus is the Messiah, the son of God...."*

John finishes with Jesus' appearance to the disciples in Galilee while they were fishing. Like Mary, none of them recognized him at first. It is here that John is identified as being the disciple whom Jesus loved: *"It is this same disciple who is the witness to these things; it is he who wrote them down and his testimony, we know, is true."*

INCONSISTENCIES AND DISCREPANCIES

There are many confusing issues raised by these accounts. How many people first went to the tomb? When was the stone rolled back from the entrance? How many angels were involved? Did Jesus appear at the tomb? How did the disciples react when they heard the news? Why didn't Mary Magdalene, and later all the disciples, recognize Jesus after his resurrection? How often did he appear before ascending to heaven?

There are too many inconsistencies among all of these narratives. In an event so important to the basic doctrines of the religion, they lead to serious concern. Certainly, if we depend on the New Testament alone, we can never know what really happened.

One especially serious discrepancy stands out: how many days elapsed between the crucifixion and the resurrection of Jesus?

> ... *"An evil and unfaithful age is eager for a sign!*
> *No sign will be given it but that of the prophet Jonah.*
> *Just as Jonah spent three days and*
> *three nights in the belly of the whale,*
> *so will the Son of Man spend three days*
> *and three nights in the bowels of the earth."*
> **[Matthew 12:39-40]**

> *The next day, the one following the Day of Preparation,*
> *the chief priests and the Pharisees called at Pilate's residence.*
> *"Sir," they said, "We have recalled that that imposter*
> *while he was still alive made the claim,*
> *'After three days I will rise.'"*
> **[Matthew 27:62-63]**

> *He began to teach them that the Son of Man*
> *had to suffer much, be rejected by the elders,*
> *the chief priests, and the scribes, be put to death,*
> *and rise three days later.*
> **[Mark 8:31]**

According to all four gospels, Jesus was crucified on Friday, and resurrected Sunday morning. This amounts to less than two days, and two nights. The discrepancy is obvious; Jesus was not in the grave *"for three days and three nights."*

There is also some confusion about how early the resurrection could have taken place. In John's narration, it was still dark when Mary Magdalene first went to the tomb. In other narrations, it was after sunrise. In any case, it seems clear that the common Christian idea of the resurrection at sunrise is impossible.

Many Christian scholars believe that the resurrection of Jesus was not "a physical resurrection," but a spiritual one. For example, in discussing the views of the early Alexandrian theologian Origen, Robert M. Grant states in his book *THE EARLIEST LIVES OF JESUS* (Harper & Brothers, 1961, p. 78):

> Origen's position in regard to the resurrection of Jesus, the cardinal and undeniable miracle, is not ambiguous, though it seemed so to literalists in antiquity. There is reason to suppose that he did not regard the resurrection of Jesus as "physical" — but at the same time he undoubtedly regarded it as historical.

THE QURAN'S ACCOUNT OF RESURRECTION

Fortunately, we now possess the first tangible proof regarding, among other things, the resurrection of Jesus. I am referring, of course, to the mathematically authenticated statements of the Quran, the Final Testament. As discussed in the last chapter, we learn from this numerically structured scripture that all the righteous are alive at their Lord. They are waiting in the same Paradise that Adam and Eve were in until just before the Day of Resurrection. On that day:

> *The horn is blown, whereupon everyone*
> *in the heavens and the earth is struck dead,*
> *except those whom God wills. Then it is blown again,*
> *whereupon they rise up, looking.*
> *Then the earth shines with the light of its Lord.*
> *The record is presented, and the prophets*
> *and the witnesses are brought forth.*
> *Then everyone is judged equitably, without the least injustice.*
> **[Quran 39:68-69]**

It is from this taste of death that the righteous will be resurrected. Jesus' resurrection will take place, along with everyone else's, on the Day of Resurrection. This is described as a specific eternal day that will come after this world has ended.

According to both the Quran and the Bible, death will be abolished, this world will be terminated and then new heavens and earth will be created:

*Then I saw new heavens and a new earth.
The former heavens and the former earth
had passed away, and the sea was no longer.*
                    [Revelation 21:1]

*The day will come when a new earth other than this earth,
and new heavens other than these heavens, will be substituted,
and everyone will rise up before God; the only God, the Supreme.*
                    [Quran 14:48]

The resurrection of Jesus on the universal Day of Resurrection is prominently featured in the Quran. There is just a general reference to the resurrection of all the messengers of God. Jesus is the only messenger to be mentioned by name in connection with that day.

Here is the verse mentioning all of the messengers:

*(On the Day of Resurrection)
God will gather all the messengers and say to them,
"How was the response to you?"
They will say, "We know not;
You are the only knower of all secrets."*
                    [Quran 5:109]

Immediately following this, Jesus is given special attention (5:110-120). Verse 5:116 specifically refers to his resurrection:

*(On the Day of Resurrection)
God will ask Jesus, the son of Mary,
"O Jesus, son of Mary, did you say to the people,
'Idolize me and my mother, as gods besides God?' "
Jesus will say, "Be You glorified, I could not possibly
say what is not right about me.
Had I said that, You would have known about it.
You know my innermost thoughts, while I know not Your thoughts;
surely, You are the knower of all secrets.
I never told them except that which You
have commanded me to say:
that you shall worship God, my Lord and your Lord.**

I was a witness among them, for as long as I lived among them.
When You terminated my life, You were the watcher over them;
You are witness to all things.
If You punish them, they are your servants,
and if You forgive them, You are the Almighty, the Most Wise."
God will say, "This is the day when the truthful
will benefit from their truthfulness."
They enjoy gardens with flowing streams, wherein they abide forever.
God is pleased with them, and they are pleased with Him.
Such is the great triumph.
[Quran 5:116-119]

The asterisk in the above quote marks a statement that is almost identical to Jesus' statement in John 20:17:

Jesus then said: "Do not cling to me,
for I have not yet ascended to the Father.
Rather, go to my brothers and tell them,
'I am ascending to my Father and your Father,
to my God and your God!'"
[John 20:17]

CONCLUSION

The various accounts in the Bible dealing with Jesus' resurrection are so full of inconsistencies that they leave the whole issue in doubt.

The Quran clears up the questions raised by these inconsistencies. It emphasizes that the only resurrection of Jesus will be on the one universal Day of Resurrection, along with every human being who ever existed in this world.

If the righteous do not die (as discussed in Chapter 13), and thus Jesus never really died, it makes sense that he cannot be resurrected until after everyone is struck dead at the end of the world and then resurrected:

The horn is blown, whereupon everyone in the heavens
and the earth is struck dead, except those whom God wills.
Then it is blown again, whereupon they rise up, looking.
[Quran 39:68]

Chapter Fifteen

WHO WAS JESUS?

> *As he entered Jerusalem the whole city*
> *was stirred to its depths,*
> *demanding, "Who is this?"*
> *And the crowd kept answering,*
> *"This is the prophet Jesus*
> *from Nazareth in Galilee."*
> **[Matthew 21:10-11]**

We have examined the traditional Christian identity of Jesus. We looked at the possibility of his being God, a part of the Trinity, the Savior of mankind and the only son of God. There is very strong evidence from both the Bible and the mathematically proven verses of the Quran against every one of these definitions.

This leaves us with the question of who Jesus was. Several times we have dealt with this in passing, but this question warrants a chapter of its own.

SPECIAL SERVANT OF GOD

Clearly Jesus was not just any man. Though fully human, he was special. He was born miraculously of a virgin. He spoke with great wisdom as a newborn infant, and indeed, was a prophet from birth:

She came with him to her family, carrying him.
They said, "O Mary, you have committed something gross.

*O descendant of Aaron, your father was not a bad man,
nor was your mother unchaste."
She pointed to him.
They said, "How can we talk with an infant in the crib?"
(The infant spoke and) said, "I am a servant of God.
He has given me the scripture, and made me a prophet.
He made me blessed wherever I go,
and enjoined me to observe the contact prayers (Salat)
and the obligatory charity (Zakat) for as long as I live.
I am to obey my mother;
He did not make me a disobedient rebel.
And peace be upon me the day I was born,
the day I die, and the day I get resurrected."*
[Quran 19:27-33]

Unlike other messengers and prophets of God, there is no mention in the Bible or the Quran of his ever committing any sin.

He worked great miracles—even imparting life to clay birds and resurrecting the dead—by God's leave:

*Men of Israel, listen to me!
Jesus the Nazorean was a man whom God sent to you
with miracles, wonders and signs as his credentials.
These God worked through him in your midst,
as you well know.*
[Acts 2:22]

The teachings he brought are among the most beautiful ever given to mankind. If we all followed what he preached, the world would be a very wonderful place—heaven on earth—and the Kingdom of God which he announced would have indeed come to our planet:

*The scribe said to him: "Excellent, Teacher!
You are right in saying,
'He is the One, there is no other than He.'
Yes, 'to love him with all our heart,
with all our thoughts and with all our strength,*

> *and to love our neighbor as ourselves'*
> *is worth more than any burnt offering or sacrifice."*
> *Jesus approved the insight of this answer and told him,*
> *"You are not far from the reign of God."*
> **[Mark 12:32-34]**

MESSIAH

Jesus was the Messiah for whom the Jews waited. Though some Bible scholars have questioned whether Jesus ever claimed to be the Messiah, it is quite clear in the Gospel of John when Jesus was speaking to the Samaritan woman at the well:

> *The woman said to him: "I know there is a Messiah coming."*
> *(This term means Anointed.)*
> *"When he comes, he will tell us everything."*
> *Jesus replied, "I who speak to you am he."*
> **[John 4:25-26]**

Here we also see that the Messiah is defined as the Anointed one—not, as many Christians assume, Savior. The footnote for this verse in the *NEW AMERICAN BIBLE* explains that the Samaritans were not expecting a messianic king, but a prophet like Moses.

The Quran also uses the term as Anointed:

> *The angels said, "O Mary, God gives you good news*
> *of a Word from Him whose name shall be*
> *'The Messiah, Jesus, son of Mary.*
> *He will be prominent in this world and in the Hereafter,*
> *and one of those closest to Me.'"*
> **[Quran 3:45]**

MESSENGER OF GOD

As the quote given above from Acts 2:22 shows clearly, all of the signs and miracles that Jesus manifested, *"God worked through him."* Jesus always recognized that he had no real power of his own. What he did was the will of his Omnipotent Lord:

"I cannot do anything of myself.
I judge as I hear,
and my judgment is honest
because I am not seeking my own will
but the will of him who sent me."
[John 5:30]

For Jesus, doing the will of God was his whole life:
> *...The disciples were urging him, "Rabbi, eat something."*
> *But he told them:*
> *"I have food to eat of which you do not know."*
> *...Jesus explained to them:*
> *"Doing the will of him who sent me*
> *and bringing his work to completion is my food."*
> **[John 4:31-34]**

When Jesus taught, he made it clear that what he said did not come from him, but from God:
> *"For I have not spoken on my own;*
> *no, the Father who sent me has commanded me*
> *what to say and how to speak."*
> **[John 12:49]**

> *"He who does not love me does not keep my words.*
> *Yet the word you hear is not mine;*
> *it comes from the Father who sent me."*
> **[John 14:24]**

The following quote is important not only for its content, which shows that Jesus was sent by God, but also because it is in all four Gospels:
> *Whoever welcomes me*
> *welcomes, not me, but him who sent me.*
> **[Matthew 10:40]**
> **[Mark 9:37]**
> **[Luke 9:48]**
> **[John 13:20]**

One of the clearest statements of Jesus' mission on earth is in John:
> *Jesus looked up to heaven and said:*
> *"...I have made your name known to those*
> *you gave me out of the world.*
> *These men you gave me were yours; they have kept your word.*
> *Now they realize that all you gave me comes from you.*
> *I entrusted to them the message you entrusted to me,*
> *and they received it.*
> *They have known that in truth I came from you,*
> *they have believed it was you who sent me."*
> **[John 17:1,6-8]**

The Quran tells us that as a messenger to the Children of Israel he was to proclaim:
> *"I am here to confirm the previous scripture, the Torah*
> *and to revoke certain prohibitions*
> *imposed upon you. I come to you with proof from your Lord.*
> *Therefore, you shall observe God, and obey me.*
> *God is my Lord and your Lord;*
> *you shall worship Him alone. This is a straight path."*
> **[Quran 3:50-51]**

Yes, Jesus was a great sign to the world:
> *And (recall) the one who maintained her virginity,*
> *then we blew into her from our spirit.*
> *We rendered her and her son a sign*
> *for the whole world.*
> **[Quran 21:91]**

But it is important to realize that God has told us very clearly that Jesus is a messenger. He has also told us that we must not make distinctions among the messengers:
> *...(The believers) believe in God, His angels,*
> *His scripture, and His messengers:*
> *"We make no distinction among any of His messengers,"*

and they proclaim: "We hear and we obey.
Forgive us, our Lord.
To You is the ultimate destiny."
[Quran 2:285]

One of the greatest signs God gave us through Jesus is that a human being can attain a state of absolute devotion and submission to Him. All human beings have the potential of becoming that devoted, of making ourselves that pure, of surrendering ourselves that completely to the merciful will of our Creator:

All who are led by the Spirit of God
are sons of God.
[Romans 8:14]

Chapter Sixteen

EPILOGUE TO JESUS' TEACHINGS

*"Do not think that I have come to abolish
the law and the prophets.
I have come, not to abolish them, but to fulfill them.
Of this much I assure you; until heaven
and earth pass away,
not the smallest letter of the law,
not the smallest part of a letter,
shall be done away with until it all comes true."*
[Matthew 5:17-18]

Jesus knew that there was much more to be delivered to mankind than what he had taught, and that all of God's plan would be fulfilled. In John 16, when discussing the Paraclete to come, he said:

*"I have much more to tell you, but you cannot bear it now.
When he comes, however,
being the Spirit of truth he will guide you to all truth.
He will not speak on his own, but will speak only what he hears,
and will announce to you the things to come.*
[John 16:12-13]

Just as Jesus confirmed, corrected and fulfilled the previous scripture, the Quran confirms, corrects and fulfills the previous scriptures, the Torah and the Gospels. Even more significantly, the Quran consummates these scriptures and adds new material that the world was unprepared to receive prior to A.D. 600. The Quran completes an otherwise incomplete picture regarding the whole reason behind our existence.

CONSUMMATION OF PREVIOUS SCRIPTURE
The Quran confirms and consummates the previous scriptures. This is clearly documented in its Chapter 5:

> *We have sent down the Torah,*
> *containing guidance and light.*
> *In accordance with it, the prophets of Israel*
> *who were devoted to God, judged,*
> *as well as the rabbis and the scribes,*
> *who were entrusted with God's scripture,*
> *and were witnesses thereof.*
> *You shall not reverence humans, and reverence Me instead,*
> *and do not trade away My revelations for a cheap material gain.*
> *Those who judge not according to God's revelations,*
> *they are the unbelievers.*
> **[Quran 5:44]**

> *Subsequently, we sent Jesus, the son of Mary,*
> *confirming the Torah.*
> *We gave him the Gospel, containing guidance*
> *and light, and confirming the Torah,*
> *and providing guidance and enlightenment for the righteous.*
> **[Quran 5:46]**

> *Then we sent down to you this scripture, containing the truth,*
> *and confirming the previous scriptures*
> *and consummating them....*
> **[Quran 5:48]**

QURAN'S TEACHING ON GOD & THE ANGELS
Note the plural tense in the above quoted verses: *"we sent Jesus,"* and

"we send down to you this scripture." Dr. Rashad Khalifa explains this (*QURAN: THE FINAL TESTAMENT*, Ibid., p. 656), "Whenever the first person plural form is used by the Almighty, it invariably indicates participation of other entities, such as the angels."

According to the Quran, there was a time when only God existed, and nothing else. Then God created the angels to carry out certain functions where His physical presence is not required, or would be utterly devastating. For example, it is clearly pointed out that, although God is in full control of every atom in the universe, He is not physically present here on this earth:

*When Moses came for an audience
and his Lord spoke to him, he said,
"My Lord, allow me to look at You; allow me to see You."
God said, "You will not see Me, but look at the mountain:
if it stays in its place, then you can see Me."
Then, when his Lord manifested Himself to the mountain,
He caused it to shatter, and Moses fell unconscious.
When he came to, he said,
"Be You glorified, I repent; I am the first believer."*
[Quran 7:143]

No place in our universe can stand the immense energy and power of the physical presence of God. Consequently, all affairs in this innermost universe are conducted by the angels, in accordance with God's plan and within His full control.

SATAN'S REBELLION
The Quran clearly states that the angels were all created with full freedom to serve God or refuse to do so. Of course, in refusing to serve Him, they would be going against the divine law of His absolute sovereignty.

Like all other laws, this divine law would not be demonstrated without at least one attempted violation. For example, if there is a law stipulating that you must stay in a room, this law will not be known unless you

Epilogue to Jesus' Teachings

attempt to leave and are forced back. If you stay in the room, without ever trying to leave, there is no demonstration of the law.

One of the angels did choose to violate the law, and rebelled against God's absolute sovereignty. Satan, also known as Lucifer or Iblees, is reported in the Bible and Quran as being this angel who became infatuated with his God given powers. He was infatuated to the point of believing that he could be a god besides his Creator.

The Quran emphasizes that the universe would be utterly ruined if there were more than one God:

To God belongs everyone in the heavens and the earth.
Those at Him are never too arrogant to serve Him,
nor do they ever regret it.
They glorify Him, night and day, without ever tiring.
Have these found any other gods who
can resurrect the dead from the earth?
If the heavens and the earth had any other gods
besides the one God, they would be ruined.
God be glorified, He is the One with total authority,
high above anything they describe.
He is not to be asked about His actions,
but everyone else must be asked.
If they set up other gods, then say, "Show us your proof!"
[Quran 21:19-24]

EARTH AS SATAN'S DOMINION

God informed Satan that he was not capable of ruling as a god. The Quran tells us that God backed this up with a practical demonstration. When a statement like "you are not capable of ruling as a god" is made, the way to prove it is to allow the claimant to try being a god.

God told Satan that He would set up a temporary kingdom for him to rule, and thus demonstrate Satan's incompetence. In providing Satan with a dominion, it is quite obvious that God went out of His way to ridicule Satan's projected dominion in relation to His own. Thus, He created seven vast universes (see Chapter 8), and created in the innermost universe a billion trillion stars. One of the smaller stars in the smallest universe was surrounded by a dozen planets, one of them the planet Earth. It is on this insignificant speck in the smallest universe that Satan is to demonstrate his abilities as a god.

A successful god would rule over a 'perfect' kingdom: a kingdom where there are no diseases, no accidents, no misery; where all constituents enjoy perfect health, wealth, peace and happiness.

This is what God promises those who choose Him as their King:

It is not for you to be in search of what you are to eat or drink.
Stop worrying. The unbelievers of this world
are always running after these things.
Your Father knows that you need such things.
Seek out instead his kingship over you,
and the rest will follow in turn.
[Luke 12:29-31]

God promises those who believe and lead a righteous life,
that He will make them sovereigns on earth,
as He did for those before them,
and He will strengthen for them the religion
He has prescribed for them,
and He will substitute, in place of their worries,
happiness and security.
All this, if they worship Me alone,
without setting up any idols besides Me....
[Quran 24:55]

Absolutely, God's allies have nothing to fear, nor will they grieve.
They are those who believe and lead a righteous life.
Their lot is happiness in this world, as well as in the Hereafter.
This is God's inviolable law.
Such is the greatest triumph.
[Quran 10:62-64]

The Bible, in Matthew, and even more clearly in Luke, demonstrates that Satan is the king of this world:

*Then the devil took him (Jesus) up higher
and showed him all the kingdoms of the world in a single instant.
He said to him, "I will give you all this power and
the glory of these kingdoms;
the power has been given to me and I give it to whomever I wish.
Prostrate yourself in homage before me, and it shall all be yours."*
[Luke 4:5-7]

THE HUMAN'S ROLE

But what about the constituents of Satan's minute kingdom? How did we end up here?

Rashad Khalifa explained the whole issue in the introduction to his final translation of the Quran (projected publication date 1991):

> It all began billions of years ago when one of God's high-ranking creatures, Satan, developed a supercilious idea that he could run a dominion as an independent god besides God. This challenge to God's absolute authority was not only blasphemous, it was also erroneous. Satan was ignorant of the fact that God alone possesses the ability to be a god, and that there is much more to godhood than he realized. It was the ego – arrogance augmented by ignorance – that led Satan to believe that he could take care of a dominion, as a god, and run it without disease, misery, war, accidents, and chaos. The vast majority of God's creatures disagreed with Satan. Yet, the minute egotistic minority that agreed with him to various extents were in the billions. Thus, a profound dispute erupted within the Heavenly Community (38:69). The rebels' unjustifiable challenge to God's absolute authority was met and resolved in the most efficient manner. After giving the rebels sufficient chances to renounce their crime and submit to Him, God decided to exile the hard core rebels on a space ship called Earth, and give them yet another chance to redeem themselves.... Those who agreed with Satan...were given a chance to kill their egos and submit to God's absolute authority. While the vast majority of the guilty creatures took advantage of this opportunity, a minuscule minority consisting of about 150 billion creatures failed to take advantage of this offer (33:72).

We are among those who did not take advantage of that offer to submit. Khalifa goes on to describe the division of all of God's creatures into four classifications as a result of this feud.

The angels are those creatures who never questioned God's absolute authority. This group makes up the vast majority. The Quran tells us that the size of this group is so great that only God knows their number (74:31).

The next category are those creatures who accepted God's offer to submit and return to His dominion. They chose to renounce free will, kill their egos and come to this world in a submissive role:

*We have offered the responsibility (freedom of choice)
to the heavens and the earth, and the mountains,
but they refused to bear it, and were afraid of it.
But the human being accepted it; he was transgressing, ignorant.*
[Quran 33:72]

All creatures within our universe, except humans and their jinn companions, fall into this category. This also includes humans who die as children, or are retarded and obviously unable to exercise free will. These beings are redeemed back into God's eternal kingdom by their acceptance of submissive roles.

The final two categories, humans and jinns, are interrelated. Dr. Khalifa gives so much valuable information on these two critical groups that I will again quote from him:

(3) The Humans

The hard-core rebels — humans and jinns — refused to denounce their crime, and opted for witnessing a demonstration of Satan's claim. These egotistic creatures who failed to submit to God's absolute authority, even when offered a chance to do so, were divided in half. The half that were less convinced of Satan's point of view became classified as humans. Although they harbored doubts about Satan's claim, they failed to make a firm stand regarding God's absolute authority. It is the ego that prevented these creatures from appreciating God's omnipotence, it is the ego that prevented them from submitting when such an opportunity was offered to them (33:72), and it is the ego that stands between most of us and redemption to God's kingdom (25:43). This is why "Kill your ego" is one of the first commandments in the Quran (2:54).

(4) The Jinns

The other half of the guilty creatures, those who leaned closer to Satan's point of view and exhibited the biggest egos, became classified as jinns. It was God's plan to assign one jinn to every human being from birth to death. The jinn companion represents Satan and constantly promotes his point of view (50:23, 27). Both the jinns and the humans are given a precious chance in this world to re-educate themselves, denounce their egoism and redeem themselves by submitting to God's absolute authority. Whenever a human being is born, a jinn is born and is assigned to the new human. We learn from the Quran that the jinns are Satan's descendants (7:27, 18:50). When a jinn being is born and assigned to a human being, the jinn remains a constant companion of the human until the human dies. The jinn is then freed, and lives on for a few centuries. Both humans and jinns are required to worship God alone (51:56).

CHILDREN OF GOD vs CHILDREN OF SATAN

The scriptures divide the human race into two groups: children of God and children of Satan. Those who do the will of God and follow His commandments are consistently called sons or children of God. Those who use their free will to avoid God and His commandments are siding with the devil; they are his children.

A complete picture of these groups emerges when we review the scriptures. Early in the Book of Genesis we note that the human soul emanated from God Himself:

*—the Lord God formed man out of the clay of the ground
and blew into his nostrils the breath of life,
and so man became a living being.*
[Genesis 2:7]

As just quoted from R. Khalifa, according to the Quran, humans are all descendants of Adam, each with a soul coming from God. Everytime one of these descendants of Adam is born, a descendant of Satan is also born. The 'newborn' descendant of Satan is attached to the newborn human and becomes a lifelong companion. So, every human has a piece of God (the soul) and a piece of Satan (the companion) within him.

Though it may sound new, this concept is not foreign to the Judeo-Christian framework. The traditional cartoon character caught between his angelic conscience sitting on his right shoulder and his satanic lust on his left is familiar to us all.

Haven't we all done something so alien to our own values and goals that we can't believe that it came from us?

This concept is also closely paralleled in the *Manual of Discipline,* one of the Dead Sea Scrolls. The following is quoted from Theodor H. Gaster's compilation and translation of the scrolls *(THE DEAD SEA SCRIPTURES,* Third edition, 1976, pp. 48-49). The *Manual of Discipline* laid down the rules for all the members of an esoteric Jewish community in existence at the time of Christ's birth and has this to say about the two representatives:

> ...God created man to rule the world, and appointed for him two spirits after whose direction he was to walk until the final Inquisition. They are the spirits of truth and of perversity.
>
> The origin of truth lies in the Fountain of Light, and that of perversity in the Wellspring of Darkness. All who practice righteousness are under the domination of the Prince of Lights, and walk in ways of light; whereas all who practice perversity are under the domination of the Angel of Darkness and walk in ways of darkness. Through the Angel of Darkness, however, even those who practice righteousness are made liable to error. All their sin and their iniquities, all their guilt and their deeds of transgression are the result of his domination; and this, by God's inscrutable design, will continue until the time appointed by Him.

According to the Quran, throughout the life of every human being, Satan's representative, the jinn, does his job of trying to convince the human soul, i.e., the real person, that God's commandments need not be followed. This is precisely what the Bible tells us Adam and Satan went through; Satan duped Adam and Eve into breaking God's law, as symbolized by the forbidden tree:

> ...*The serpent asked the woman, "Did God really*
> *tell you not to eat from any of the trees in the garden?"*
> *The woman answered the serpent:*
> *"We may eat of the fruit of the trees of the garden;*
> *it is only about the fruit of the tree*
> *in the middle of the garden that God said,*
> *'You shall not eat it or even touch it, lest you die.' "*
> *But the serpent said to the woman: "You certainly will not die!*
> *No, God knows well that the moment you eat of it*
> *you will be like gods who know what is good and what is bad."*
> *The woman saw that the tree was good for food,*
> *pleasing to the eyes, and desirable for gaining wisdom.*
> *So she took some of its fruit and ate it;*
> *and she also gave some to her husband,*
> *who was with her, and he ate it.*
> *Then the eyes of both of them were opened,*
> *and they realized that they were naked;*
> **[Genesis 3:1-7]**

This concept of our satanic jinn companion is new, and perhaps strange for many. However, it clarifies an otherwise puzzling passage in the Book of Matthew. When Jesus started to prepare his disciples for his impending crucifixion, Peter protested that Jesus might be spared. Jesus reacted strongly:

> *Jesus turned on Peter and said, "Get out of my sight, you satan!*
> *You are trying to make me trip and fall.*
> *You are not judging by God's standards but by man's."*
> **[Matthew 16:23]**

We are constantly dealing with our satanic companion who is trying to influence us to follow Satan's urgings rather than God's commandments. The scriptures clearly state that those of us who follow Satan's urgings are children of Satan, while those who follow God's commandments are God's children. Following God's commandments results in the growth and development of the godly entity, the real human person (the soul). Thus, any human being, whether perceived by this person or not, is either a child of God, or a child of the devil, depending on which entity has grown and developed. This is exactly what Jesus taught:

> *They cried, "We are no illegitimate breed!*
> *We have but one father and that is God himself."*
> *Jesus answered: "Were God your father you would love me,*
> *for I came forth from God, and am here.*
> *I did not come of my own will; it was he who sent me.*
> *Why do you not understand what I say?*
> *It is because you cannot bear to hear my word.*
> *The father you spring from is the devil,*
> *and willingly you carry out his wishes...."*
> **[John 8:41-44]**

So here we have it—the reason for our existence: We are here to try to kill our egos, convert our jinn companions, submit fully to God alone, and thus redeem ourselves back into His kingdom.

HOW DO WE GET BACK?

What exactly do we need to do to redeem ourselves back to God? Clearly, there is not just one path to follow:

> *Surely, those who believe, those who are Jewish,*
> *the Christians, the converts; anyone who*
> *(1) believes in God, and*
> *(2) believes in the Hereafter, and*
> *(3) leads a righteous life,*
> *will receive their recompense from their Lord;*
> *they have nothing to fear, nor will they grieve.*
> **[Quran 2:62 & 5:69]**

The issue is not what you call yourself—Jew, Christian, Buddhist, Muslim, etc. The issue is devotion to God alone, of worshiping God as Jesus and all of God's messengers taught:

> *"...You shall love the Lord your God*
> *with all your heart,*
> *with all your soul,*
> *with all your mind,*
> *and with all your strength."*
> **[Mark 12:30]**

This automatically precludes associating anything with God—and this is the difficult thing for human beings. We are idolatrous by nature. That is why we are here in the first place. If we did not have the tendency to associate idols with God we would have stood solidly with Him in the heavenly feud instead of leaning toward Satan's point of view.

GOD'S HELP

The Quran tells us that, in spite of our continued rebellion, God, in His great mercy, gave us the natural instinct to worship Him alone before we were sent to this testing ground:

> *Recall that your Lord summoned all the descendants of Adam,*
> *and had them bear witness for themselves: "Am I not your Lord?"*
> *They all said, "Yes. We bear witness."*
> *Thus, you cannot say on the Day of Resurrection,*
> *"We were not aware of this."*
> *Nor can you say, "It was our parents who practiced idolatry,*
> *and we simply followed in their footsteps.*
> *Will You punish us for the sins of the innovators?"*
> *We thus explain the revelations, to enable them to return.*
> **[Quran 7:172-174]**

Besides this, God has sent prophets and messengers again and again to warn the people and deliver good news to those who do devote themselves totally to God. Whenever the message has been corrupted beyond recognition, it has been renewed. The Quran is such a renewal.

It is the final scripture. Perhaps that is why it is guarded by its miraculous numerical code.

We know that all the prophets and messengers brought one and the same message: Worship God alone. Following this message is not always easy. We must fight against Satan, and his descendants—one of whom is our own constant companion. We must fight against our own egos.

We must convert our companion to God's point of view. And we must kill our own ego. Essentially, we must diminish the power of the piece of Satan within us (which is our companion) and we must increase the power of the piece of God within us (our soul).

How do we cause our souls to grow? We must obey God's commands and do righteous works. All faiths have their own rituals, but God gave mankind a specific set of especially powerful practices through the father of monotheistic religion, Abraham. To some degree or another these practices still survive in Judaism, Christianity and Islam. The Quran talks about each of these practices.

ABRAHAM'S RELIGION

The most important practice is the contact prayers. These prayers are a specific set of words and motions to be performed five times a day at specific times. The words are simple, and turn out to be also mathematically composed. In fact, all aspects of the prayer are tied to the code, from the number of prayers recited, to the words themselves, and the number of units in each prayer. Though each prayer takes only a few minutes, it brings the soul into actual contact with God, and causes enormous growth.

The universal nature of this practice is seen in the fact that the prayers of the Samaritan Jews are almost identical to those discussed in the Quran, though said in Hebrew rather than Arabic. Among Christians the words have been lost, but the motions of a priest giving the Mass are almost the same as those of the contact prayer. Before the contact prayer is performed, the worshiper performs a symbolic ablution. This practice is also a common one, and may be the origin of the practice of baptism.

The second practice given through Abraham is a purification charity. Two and one-half percent of one's net income must be given to the poor on the day it is received. The recipients begin with one's own parents and family. If the family is not in need, the charity goes to orphans, the traveling alien and the poor, in that order. This charity is the right of the recipients, and is given to purify one's income. Of course, charity is also an integral part of all faiths.

The third practice given to Abraham is fasting during a specified month of the year. The fast is observed from the earliest light of dawn to sunset. Nothing is taken into the body during this time period (except in health emergencies). In what are probably modified observances of this same practice, Jews observe a complete fast for twenty-four hours on the Day of Atonement. Christians have modified this to a forsaking of a special food during Lent, though some denominations still do observe fasts, and others do not observe either fasts or giving up foods at Lent.

The last practice is to go on a pilgrimage once in one's lifetime, if one is able, to commemorate Abraham's submission to God, and God's redemption of him and his son.

These simple but powerful practices nourish the soul greatly. We cannot picture the degree of that nourishment, but God tells us that just the charity alone is like *"a grain that produces seven spikes, with a hundred grains in each spike."* (Quran 2:261) In other words, we are rewarded for our charities an equivalent of seven hundred times what we give.

HEAVEN AND HELL

The Quran tells us very clearly that the descriptions of heaven and hell in the scriptures are allegorical (47:15 and 2:24-26). If the soul is strong, it can withstand the immense energy and power of God, and being in His presence is heaven. For weak souls, being in the presence of God is painful, and they will run as far away from God as possible to escape that pain. Separation from God is hell.

Thus we see that each of us determines our own position. God does not put anyone in hell; they run there to escape the greater pain of being in

God's presence. This stratification of souls in the Hereafter is mentioned in the Bible:

> *...Whoever breaks the least significant*
> *of these commands and teaches others to do so*
> *shall be called least in the kingdom of God.*
> *Whoever fulfills and teaches these commands*
> *shall be great in the kingdom of God.*
> **[Matthew 5:19]**

> *Then they who fear the Lord spoke with one another,*
> *and the Lord listened attentively;*
> *and a record book was written before him*
> *of those who fear the Lord and trust in his name.*
> *And they shall be mine, says the Lord of hosts,*
> *my own special possession, on the day I take action.*
> *And I will have compassion on them*
> *as a man has compassion on his son who serves him.*
> *Then you will again see the distinction between*
> *the just and the wicked;*
> *between him who serves God,*
> *and him who does not serve him.*
> **[Malachi 3:16-18]**

CONCLUSION

Now, with our added knowledge from the Quran, we realize that any who do not serve God alone are enslaved by Satan.

Our existence is not a simple matter. We are here in this life as a final chance to renounce all forms of idolatry, to return to the pristine worship of God alone—to love God with all our heart, all our soul, all our mind, all our strength. If we are not successful, we will be doomed by our lack of growth to exile from God—to hell. If we are successful, then the following good news is for us:

> *You have no idea how much joy and happiness*
> *are waiting for you as a reward for your (righteous) works.*
> **[Quran 32:17]**

APPENDIX

REFERENCES

INDEX

APPENDIX:

THE QURAN'S MATHEMATICAL CODE

THE CODE — SIMPLE FACTS

1. There are 114 chapters in the Quran, or 19 x 6.

2. The total number of verses in the Quran is 6346, or 19 x 334.

3. When you add the 30 different numbers which are mentioned in the Quran's text: 1, 2, 3, 4, 5, 6, 7, 8, 9, 10, 11, 12, 19, 20, 30, 40, 50, 60, 70, 80, 99, 100, 200, 300, 1000, 2000, 3000, 5000, 50000 and 100000 (i.e. one God, two brothers, etc.), the total is 162146 or 19 x 8534.

4. The first statement in Quran, "In the name of God, Most Gracious, Most Merciful" consists of 19 Arabic letters. Known as the *'Basmalah,'* it prefaces every chapter except Chapter 9.

5. Though missing from Chapter 9, exactly 19 chapters later the Basmalah occurs twice. Chapter 27 has this statement at its beginning and in verse 30. This makes the total number of times the Basmalah occurs in the Quran 114, or 19 x 6.

6. It follows that since there are 19 chapters between the missing Basmalah and the extra one, that the sum of those chapter numbers is a multiple of 19. (The sum of any 19 consecutive numbers is a multiple of 19.) But the total, 342, is also the exact number of words between the two occurrences of the Basmalah in Chapter 27. This number, 342, is 19 x 18.

7. Each word in the Basmalah occurs in the Quran a number of times which is a multiple of 19.
   —The first word "Ism" (name) occurs 19 times.
   —The second word "Allah" (God) occurs 2698 times or 19 x 142.
   —The third word "Al-Rahman" (Most Gracious) occurs 57 times or 19 x 3.
   —The fourth word "Al-Raheem" (Most Merciful) occurs 114 times or 19 x 6.
8. The first revelation that came to the prophet Mohammed, was 19 words.
9. The total number of letters in the 19 words of the first revelation is 76, 19 x 4.
10. Although they were first in order of revelation, these verses are placed at the beginning of Chapter 96 in the final order of compilation. This chapter is atop the last 19 chapters.
11. Chapter 96 consists of 304 Arabic letters, or 19 x 16. And those 304 letters make up 19 verses.
12. The last chapter revealed (Chapter 110) has 19 words, and its first verse is 19 letters.
13. As mentioned above, the word *"Allah"* (God) occurs 2698 times (19 x 142). If you add the numbers of the verses where this word occurs, the total is 118123 or 19 x 6217.
14. The main message in the Quran is that there is only 'One God'. The number of times that the word *"Wahed"* (one) is used to refer to this concept of One God is 19.
15. At the time of the revelation of the Quran letters were used as numbers, in the same way that the Romans used their letters, now known as Roman numerals. The importance of the concept of One God is underscored by the fact that if you take the numerical values assigned to the letters of *"Wahed"*: $W = 6$, $A = 1$, $H = 8$, $D = 4$, the total is 19. These values are known as the gematrical value of

the letters. It is very interesting that the gemetrical value for the Hebrew word "one" or "*Vahed*" is also 19.

16. The word "Quran," in all of its grammatical forms, occurs in 38 different chapters (38 is 19 x 2). When you exclude any occurrences where it refers to a Quran other than the actual Quran which we have (for example, one excluded verse refers to a hypothetical non-Arabic Quran), and add the chapter and verse numbers for those occurrences, the total is 4408, or 19 x 232.

17. The total number of times "the Quran" is mentioned is 58 times, but one of them refers to "a Quran other than this" which the disbelievers demanded. So the actual number of references to the actual book the Quran is 57 or 19 x 3.

18. Within the 114 chapters of the Quran, 29 of them are prefixed with certain letters of the Arabic alphabet, or 'Quranic initials.' Intermixed between the first initialed chapter (Chapter 2) and the last initialed chapter (Chapter 68), there are 38 non-initialed chapters, or 19 x 2.

19. In this same group of chapters, from Chapter 2 to Chapter 68, there are 19 alternating sets of initialed and non-initialed chapters.

20. The total number of verses making up this group of chapters is 5263, 19 x 277.

21. Within this group of chapters there are also 2641 occurrences of the word '*Allah*', or 19 x 139. Of course, that leaves 57, or 19 x 4, occurrences of that word outside of this group.

22. If you add the chapter and verse numbers of the 57 occurrences of '*Allah*' outside the initialed section, the total is 2432 or 19 x 128.

QURANIC INITIALS

As we discussed in Chapter Ten, it was the search for an explanation of the Quranic Initials which led to the discovery of the code imbedded in the Arabic text of this scripture. These initials exhibit many aspects of the code, when looked at as individual sets and when looked at all

198 JESUS: MYTH & MESSAGE

together. In Chapter Ten we examined some of the Quranic Initials. Here we will look at all of them.

Let us begin by looking at the initials which use a single letter. The first one we will examine is the initial which has the English transliteration of 'Q'.

THE INITIAL 'Q.' (Qaaf)

There are several special phenomena having to do with the initial Q. Perhaps it can be seen as standing for Quran. This is especially so since there are two Q-initialed chapters, each with 57 (19 x 3) Q's in them. Thus the total of Q's in both chapters is 114 (19 x 6), the same number as the number of chapters in the Quran.

The fact that both Q-initialed chapters contain exactly 57 Q's is quite remarkable because the first of them (Chapter 42) is more than twice as long as the second (Chapter 50).

There is another remarkable phenomenon in the sum of the number of each chapter with the number of verses in that chapter. Chapter 42 has 53 verses; 42 plus 53 is 95, 19 x 5. If we look at the other Q-initialed chapter, 50, it has 45 verses; 50 plus 45 is also 95.

Dr. Khalifa's idea that Q might stand for the Quran is strengthened by discoveries made after his assassination (*SUBMITTERS PERSPECTIVE*, Masjid Tucson, December, 1990). When you look at the chapters between and inclusive of those Q initialed chapters (Chapters 42 and 53) there are some interesting facts. First of all, the total number of Q's occurring in that group of chapters is 456, or 19 times 24.

Also, if you add the total number of verses in these 9 chapters you have 403. This number added to the sum of the chapter numbers, 414, is 817, or 19 times 43.

Then, if you look at the gematrical value of the initials in the initializing verses for those chapters, the total is 570 or 19 times 30.

Finally, let us examine the chapter numbers and verse numbers for the six occurrences of the word 'Quran' in those chapters (42:7; 43:3 & 31;

46:29; 47:24 and 50:1). When you add just the chapter numbers: 42 + 43 + 46 + 47 + 50, the total is 228, or 19 times 12. Likewise, when you add the verse numbers: 7 + 3 + 31 + 29 + 24 + 1, the total is 95, or 19 times 5.

THE INITIAL 'N.' (Noon)

This initial prefixes only one chapter, number 68. Chapter 68 is the last initialed chapter. In the case of this one initial only, the letter's name is spelled out in the Arabic—*Noon Wow Noon*. The total number of occurrences of N in this chapter, including the two occurrences in the initial's name, is 133, or 19 x 7.

THE INITIAL 'Š.' (Saad)

Š prefixes three different chapters, 7, 19 and 38. The total occurrences of Š in these three chapters taken together is 152, or 19 x 8.

At this point it should probably be mentioned again, as it was mentioned in Chapter Nine, that Dr. Khalifa could not ignore the implications of the mathematical structure in the Quran, which clearly demands the rejection of any traditional Muslim teachings, not based directly on the Quran, as sources of religious guidance. The fury of the traditional clergy at his conclusions and his straightforward statement of them, eventually led to his assassination.

It is to be expected then, that those same clergy have attacked the discoveries. Most of those attacks have been focused on the Quranic Initials, and one of their major arguments is with the 'Saad.' This is because in modern copies of the Quran the Arabic word "*Bastatan*" is written with a 'Saad' rather than 'Seen.' This would increase the count of 'Saad' by one, and it would no longer be divisible by 19. But the oldest available copy of the Quran, the Tashkent copy, writes "*Bastatan*" with a "Seen." Dr. Khalifa includes a reproduction from that Tashkent copy in his translation (*QURAN: THE FINAL TESTAMENT*, 1989, p. 614).

In most cases, the initials occur together in sets. Next, we will examine some of these sets.

THE INITIALS 'Y.S.' (Ya Seen)
These two initials are found at the beginning of Chapter 36. The number of times that these two letters appear in this chapter is 285, or 19 x 15.

The Quran uses two different forms of 'Y' one of which is very subtle for non-Arabic readers to distinguish. Khalifa's book QURAN: VISUAL PRESENTATION OF THE MIRACLE (Islamic Productions, 1982) shows every 'Y' and 'S' marked in the Arabic text of Chapter 36.

THE INITIALS 'H.M.' (Haa Meem)
This set of initials is found initializing the seven consecutive chapters 40 through 46. The total occurrence of these two in all of these chapters is 2147, or 19 x 113.

THE INITIALS 'Á.S.Q.' (Ayn Seen Qaf)
Chapter 42 is the only chapter with a set of initials (H.M.) in the first verse and another (Á.S.Q.) in verse two. Of course, the H's and M's figure in the counts for 'H.M' as mentioned above. The number of times the letters of the second set of initials, Á.S.Q., are in Chapter 42 is 209, or 19 x 11.

THE INITIALS 'A.L.M.' (Alef Laam Mim)
'A' is the most common letter in Arabic, 'L' is the second most common, and 'M' is the third most common. This combination of initials prefix six chapters: 2, 3, 29, 30, 31 and 32. In every one of those six chapters, the total occurrence of A's plus L's and M's is divisible by 19. Of course this means that when looking at all six chapters together, the grand total of all these initials is divisible by 19.

THE INITIALS 'A.L.R.' (Alef Laam Ra)
These initials prefix Chapters 10, 11, 12, 14 and 15. Again, in each of those chapters the total number of A's plus L's plus R's is divisible by 19.

INITIALS 'A.L.M.R' (Alef Laam Mim Ra)
This group of initials prefix only Chapter 13. Their total combined frequency in that chapter is 1482, or 19 times 78.

INITIALS 'A.L.M.Š.' (Alem Laam Mim Saad)
Chapter 7 is the only chapter prefixed by this combination of initials. The total occurrence of these combined letters in this chapter is 5320, or 19 times 280.

Note that the initial Saad also interacts with the Saads of Chapters 19 and 38 to produce a total of Saads which is divisible. (See the discussion of the Initial Saad above.)

INITIALS 'K.H.Y.Á.Š.' (Kaaf Ha Ya 'Ayn Saad)
This longest set of initials begins Chapter 19. The joint total of these initials in that chapter is 798, or 19 times 42.

INITIALS 'H.' (Ha); 'T.H.' (Ta Ha); 'T.S.' (Ta Seen); and 'T.S.M.' (Ta Seen Mim)
These remaining four groups of initials interact in an interlocking and overlapping relationship which produces a combined total of 1767 which is 19 times 93.

MATHEMATICAL PROPERTIES OF THE INITIALED SURAS AS A WHOLE
Half of the Arabic alphabet, or 14 letters, are combined in various different ways to make up 14 different sets of initials. These 14 sets initializes 29 different chapters. If you take the gematrical values of each of the 14 different letters occurring as initials and sum them, you get 693. Add to that 29 for the number of chapters and you get 722, or 19 times 19 times 2.

Also, if you add the gematrical values of each initial (693 again) to the chapter numbers where each first occurs (totaling to 295) you get 988, or 19 times 52. For example, 'Alef' has the gemetrical value of 1 and first occurs in Chapter 2; 'Ha' has the gemetrical value of 5 and it first occurs in Chapter 19...those numbers for all 14 initials give you the total of 988.

You will find more of these relationships in Rashad Khalifa's appendix, along with tables illustrating them. There is one more which is so remarkable that it must be included. For each initialed chapter take the chapter number, add the number of Quranic Initials which prefix it and then add the number of verses containing initials (this number will be 1 for all chapters except 42, which has initials in two verses). As an example, the first initialed chapter is Chapter 2, it has 3 Quranic Initials which occur in 1 verse. When we add 2 plus 3 plus 1 we get 6. Let us call this total the chapter total. When you sum all the chapter totals for the initialed chapters you get 931 or 19 times 49. This in itself is amazing enough, but there is more. If you multiply the chapter number by the number of initials instead of adding them, and then add the number of verses containing initials, you still get a grand total which is a multiple of 19—2052 or 19 times 108!

You can illustrate for yourself how remarkable this is by trying to duplicate it. You will see that this definitely is not a mathematical property, and clearly indicates divine arrangement.

REFERENCES

Adler, M. *HOW TO THINK ABOUT GOD.* Macmillan Publishing Co., New York, 1980.

AKHER SAA. Cairo, Egypt, January 24, 1973.

ARIZONA DAILY STAR. Tucson, Arizona, October 18, 1987.

Bacon, F. *THE WORKS OF FRANCIS BACON*, vol. vii. Edited by B. Montagu. William Pickering, London, 1831.

Beare, F.W. *THE EARLIEST RECORDS OF JESUS.* Abingdon Press, New York, 1962.

THE BIBLE OF THE WORLD. Edited by R. O. Ballou. Viking Press, 1939

Brandon, S.G.F. *JESUS AND THE ZEALOTS.* Charles Scribner's Sons, New York, 1967.

Brashler, J. *THE NAG HAMMADI LIBRARY.* Edited by J.M. Robinson. Harper and Row, San Francisco, 1977.

Browne, L. *WISDOM OF ISRAEL.* Random House, New York, 1945.

Butterworth, Eric. *THE MAGNIFICENT TOOLS OF THE MIND.* Unity Village, Missouri 64065, no date given.

THE DEAD SEA SCRIPTURES, Third edition. Edited by T.H. Gaster. Doubleday, Garden City, New York, 1967.

EARLY CHRISTIAN FATHERS. Edited by C. C. Richardson. Macmillan, New York, 1970.

Fuller, R. *INTERPRETING THE MIRACLES.* Westminster Press, 1963.

Grant, R.M. *THE EARLIEST LIVES OF JESUS.* Harper & Brothers, New York, 1961.

HOLY BIBLE—King James Version. Crusade Bible Publishers, Inc., Nashville, Tennessee, 1977.

THE HOLY BIBLE, FROM ANCIENT EASTERN MANUSCRIPTS. Translated by G. Lamsa. A. J. Holman Co., Philadelphia, 1957.

THE HOLY SCRIPTURES—According To The Masoretic Text. The Jewish Publication Society of America, Philadelphia, 1917.

Kenyon, F. *OUR BIBLE AND THE ANCIENT MANUSCRIPTS.* Harper and Brothers, New York, 1958.

Kushner, H.S. *WHEN BAD THINGS HAPPEN TO GOOD PEOPLE.* Avon Books, New York, 1981.

Lamsa, G. *GOSPEL LIGHT.* (1936 edition) A.J. Holman Co., Philadelphia, 1936.

Lamsa, G. *NEW TESTAMENT ORIGIN.* Aramaic Bible Society, Inc., St. Petersburg Beach, Florida, no date given.

Lehmann, J. *RABBI J.* Stein & Day, New York, 1971.

THE LOST BOOKS OF THE BIBLE & THE FORGOTTEN BOOKS OF EDEN. New American Library, New York, 1974.

Maccoby, H. *THE MYTHMAKER.* Harper and Row, San Francisco, 1987.

Mansour, A. *THE HISTORY OF RELIGIOUS SECTARIANISM.* The Message Publishers, Cairo, Egypt, 1985.

Marxsen, W. *JESUS AND EASTER.* Translated by V. F. Furnish. Abingdon Press, Nashville, Tennessee, 1990.

THE MYTH OF GOD INCARNATE. Edited by John Hick. The Westminster Press, Philadelphia, 1977.

THE NEW AMERICAN BIBLE. Catholic Biblical Association of America, Catholic Press, 1970.

THE NEW YORK TIMES. November 26, 1984.

QUARTERLY REVIEW. Canadian Council on the Study of Religion. April, 1983.

QURAN: THE FINAL TESTAMENT. Translated by Rashad Khalifa. Islamic Productions, Tucson, Arizona, 1989.

Sagan, Carl. *CONTACT.* Simon & Schuster, 1985.

Schaberg, J. *THE ILLEGITIMACY OF JESUS.* Harper and Row, San Francisco, 1987.

D. C. Schwarts and J. H. Glascock, *Builder,* July, 1990

SCIENTIFIC AMERICAN. September, 1980.

STRONG'S EXHAUSTIVE CONCORDANCE OF THE BIBLE.

STUDIES IN JEWISH MYSTICISM. Edited by J. Dan and F. Talmage. Association for Jewish Studies, Cambridge, Massachusetts, 1982.

SUBMITTERS PERSPECTIVE. Masjid Tucson, Tucson, Arizona, February, 1990.

Taylor, V. *THE NAMES OF JESUS.* St. Martin's Press, New York, 1953.

Wells, G. A. *WHO WAS JESUS?* Open Court Publishing, La Salle, IL, 1989.

Wilken, R. L. *THE MYTH OF CHRISTIAN BEGINNINGS.* Doubleday, Garden City, New York, 1971.

Yates, J. *A VINDICATION OF UNITARIANISM.* Wells & Lilly, Boston, 1816.

Index

A
ablution 190
Abraham 17, 46, 131 - 132, 149, 190
Acts 19
   02:22 173 - 174
   21:20-26 51, 55
Adam 37, 68, 131 - 134, 142, 156, 169, 185, 187
Adler, M. 97 - 98
AKHERSA 120
Amram 127
angels 68 - 69, 163, 167, 179 - 180, 184
Antioch, Bishop of 50, 82
Apocalypse of Peter 158
Apocrypha 127- 28, 131, 141-142
Apostles 7 - 8, 53, 55 - 57, 64
Apostles Creed 81
Arabic 48, 113, 190
Aramaic 12 - 13, 15, 32, 48, 113
Arian controversy 81
ARIZONA DAILY STAR 32-33
Ashkenazi Hasidism 110
Athanasian Creed 79, 81
Athanasius 81

B
Bacon, F. 78
Ballou, R. O. 131
Baptism 81, 190
Basmalah 119, 121 - 122
Beare, F. W. 7 - 8, 18
Bowden, John 3
Brandon, S. G. F. 53 - 54, 57
Brashler, J. 157 - 158
Buddhism 62, 83
Butterworth, E. 85

C
Canadian Council on the Study of Religion 119
Canon 19
Carthage, Council of 19
Chalcedon, Council of 81
charity 24, 191
Children of God
   See: Sonship to God
Children of Israel 67, 70, 139, 141, 159, 176
Christianity 97, 190
Christianity & Crisis 2
Christians
   early 6 - 7, 18, 27, 50 - 52, 55 - 58, 61, 64
   Gentile 51 - 52
   Jewish 27, 51, 58
   persecution among 82
2 Chronicles
   02:5 101
   16:25-31 103
Church
   Eastern 81 - 82
   history of 18
   Jerusalem 55
   Mother 53, 58
   and social change 2

Western 81 - 82
Codex Bezae 20
Codex Sinaiticus 19
Codex Vaticanus 9, 19
Colossians
  1:1-2 38
  1:15-17 37
companion 184 - 187, 190
Constantinople, Council of 81-82
contact prayers 24, 190
Corinthians 40
  11:03-5 54
  11:18 54
  12:2-4 101
creation 99
Crucifixion 32, 91
  See also: Jesus, death of
Cupitt, D. 58, 61 - 63

D
Dan, J. 110 - 112
David 48, 89, 126, 131, 135
Day of Atonement 191
Dead Sea Scrolls 57, 186
Deuteronomy
  05:6-9 26
  06:05 5
  06:4-5 26
  10:14 101
  18:18-19 41
Divine qualities
  See : God, qualities of

E
Early Christian Fathers 50

earth 99 - 100, 104, 181 - 183
ego 183 - 184, 190
epistles
  See: Paul, epistles
Eucharist 81
Eve 131, 133, 156, 169, 187
Exodus
  04:22-23 67
  07:08-9 139
  14:15-16 140
  20:2-5 108

F
faith vs knowledge 98
fasting 191
First commandment 5, 15, 22, 25-26, 48
free will 71, 76, 88, 182, 184 - 185
freedom of choice 88, 94
Fuller, R. 138

G
Gabriel 25
Galatians 40
  1:6-8 55
  2:6-14 56
  3:10 56
  5:3-4 56
  6:4-7 89
Garden of Gethsemane 11, 29-30
Gardner, M. 118
Gaster, T. H. 186
Genesis
  02:07 185
  03:01-7 187

16:15-16 16
17:01 80
18:13-14 132
21:2-5 16
22:1-2 17
25:7-9 17
Gnosticism 19
God
  attributes of 29, 71, 80, 87, 96, 102 - 108, 180 - 181
  creations of 99, 114
  as Father 66 - 67, 69 - 71
  as Redeemer & Savior 89-91, 94
  use of the angels 179 - 180
Gospel of the Birth of Mary 127
Gospels 6-7, 60, 65, 94, 117, 178-179
  authenticity of 9
  canonization 19
  errors in 10 - 11, 20
  history of 8, 18 - 20, 73
  oral transmission 8 - 9
  variations in 9, 11, 151-154, 167
Goulder, M. 34, 37, 58, 60, 83
Grant, R. M. 169
Greco-Roman tradition 60
Greek 9, 12, 18 - 19, 69

H
Halley's comet 115
healing 143
heaven 191
Hebrew/Aramaic 12, 32, 44, 48, 190
hell 191 - 192

Hick, J. 59, 62, 83
Hippo Regius, Council of 19
Holy Spirit 25, 79, 81 - 82, 85, 147, 167
homoousion 61, 80 - 81
Hosea
  02:01 70
  13:4 90
Houlden, L. 59
Howard, L. 2
human beings 183 - 184, 189

I
icons 61, 63, 80
Ignatius, Bishop 50, 73
Immaculate conception
  See: Jesus, immaculate concep.
incarnational belief 60
Isaac 17, 131
Isaiah 90
  09:5 or 6 44
  43:3 & 11 90
  44:24 91
  46:09 80
  55:9 107
  60:16 91
Ishmael 17
Islam 24, 61, 97, 120, 190
Israel 70
  See also: Children of Israel

J
Jeremiah 46 - 47
  1:4-5 46
Jerusalem 58

Jesus
- birth of 36, 126 - 136, 141, 172
- as a child 23
- connection w/ Adam 37, 132-134
- death of 31, 87, 91, 150 - 153, 155, 157 - 159, 187
- exaltation of 28
- followed Mosaic law 22, 48
- healed 143 - 145
- immaculate conception 36, 134
- as infant 24 - 25, 130, 141, 149, 172
- as a Jew 22
- as a messenger 24, 30, 35 - 36, 41, 47, 134, 149, 170, 172, 174, 176
- as Messiah 32-33, 36, 48, 60, 174
- miracles of 137 - 138, 140 - 149, 173 - 174
- not divine 28 - 32, 34 - 35, 40, 43, 48
- as only son refuted 72 - 75, 83
- prayer of 30 - 31
- prayer to 87
- in Quran 24 - 25, 36, 47
- as rabbi 25
- resurrection of 162 - 168, 170 - 171
- as savior 87, 89-90, 94, 109, 172
- sinless 173
- as Son of Man 65, 75
- as teacher 23 - 27, 29, 72, 175
- teachings of 7, 10, 21, 25 - 29, 71 - 72, 79, 173, 178, 188 - 189
- tempted 183
- as the Word 34 - 36, 41 - 42

Jesus Seminar 32 - 33
Jews
- and Jesus 51, 57
- concept of son of God 60

jinn *See:* companion
Job 93 - 94, 97
- 01:06 69
- 01:09-12 93
- 01:20-22 93
- 24:22-23 104
- 26:7-11 103
- 36:26 103
- 38:04-7 70
- 42:10 94

John 18, 73 - 74, 166 - 167
- 01:01 35, 133
- 01:12-13 70
- 01:14 34, 73
- 01:18 73, 75
- 02:01 12
- 03:01-7 72
- 03:14-18 75
- 03:16 72
- 03:18 73
- 04:16-19 148
- 04:23-24 27
- 04:25-26 174
- 04:31-34 175
- 04:46-53 145
- 05:30 36, 175
- 07:16-18 36
- 08:40 36
- 08:41-44 188
- 08:54-58 46
- 09:35-38 15
- 09:38 16

11:25-26 33
11:41-42 31
11:41-44 147
12:44-50 35
12:49 175
13:20 175
14:06-11 42
14:20 43
14:24 175
14:28 30
15:23 43
16:12-13 178
17:01,6-8 176
17:03 80
19:16-19 153
20:17 70, 171
John of Damascus 61, 80
John the Baptist 131
Joseph 126, 135
Judah the Pious, Rabbi 110 - 114, 117 - 118
Judaism 24, 61, 97, 190
  early Christians as Jews 27
  respect for Jesus 24

K
Kenyon, F. 9 - 11
Khalifa, R. 114, 118 - 121, 123, 156, 160, 180, 183 - 184
King James Bible 11 - 16, 39 - 40, 43, 45, 70, 75
Koran
  See: Quran
Kushner, H. S. 97 - 98

L
Lamsa, G. 8, 12, 15, 27 - 28
Lazarus 147
Lehmann, Johannes 12
Lent 191
Logos 133
Lord's Prayer 9, 31, 67, 70
Lord, as a title 28, 47 - 48
LOST BOOKS OF THE BIBLE
  128, 131, 141, 143
Luke 7, 19, 73, 135
  01:28-32 126
  01:46-48 90
  01:46-50 128
  01:49-52 105
  01:7,13 132
  02:04-5 135
  02:46-49 23
  02:52 23
  03:23-38 68
  04:05-7 183
  04:14-16 23
  07:11-16 146
  08:43-46 144
  09:48 175
  10:25-28 27
  10:27 5, 22
  11:02 67
  11:1-4 31
  12:28-31 94
  12:29-31 182
  12:29-32 71
  22:42 30
  22:44 30
  23:08-11 159

23:26-34 153
23:44-47 150
24:01-12 166
footnote to 24:1 162

M
Maccoby, H. 53
Malachi
  02:10 66
  03:16-18 192
Mansour, A. 42
Manual of Discipline 186
Marcion of Sinope 19
Mark 7, 73, 165
  01:30-31 145
  01:40-42 143
  08:31 168
  09:37 175
  10:17-18 29
  10:18 37
  10:27 105
  12:29 26
  12:29-30 26
  12:30 5, 22, 189
  12:32-34 26, 174
  15:03-5 159
  15:34 32
Marxsen, W. 154, 162
Mary 24, 36, 63, 126 - 133, 135 - 136, 145
Mass 190
mathematical code 110 - 118, 120 - 125, 127, 129, 133, 138, 157, 172, 190
Matthew 7 - 8, 73, 135

01:16 135
01:18-19 135
02:1-2 13 - 14
02:7-8 14
05:17-18 178
05:17-19 28
05:19 192
06:09 67
06:9-13 31
07:21-23 28, 84
09:06-8 143
09:18-19,23-25 147
09:27-30 146
10:28-31 105
10:40 175
11:04-6 137
12:09-13 144
12:38 137
12:39-40 168
14:15-21 149
16:23 187
20:23 29
21:10-11 172
22:37 5
22:41-44 47
23:09 71
24:36 29
26:39 30
27:27-46 152
27:46 32
27:57-28:15 163 - 165
27:62-63 168
28:18-19 79
messenger, scripture as 42
Messiah 32 - 33, 36, 47, 68, 84, 126, 129, 133 - 134, 141, 159,

167, 174
Milky Way   99
miracles
   See: Jesus, miracles of
monotheism   80
Mosaic law   22, 25, 27 - 28, 48, 52-53, 55 - 57, 60, 141
Moses   138 - 140, 149, 180
Mother Church   55
   See also: Church, Jerusalem
Muhammad   149
MYTH OF GOD INCARNATE   32, 34, 38, 58 - 61, 63, 80, 83

N
Nag Hammadi Library   157 - 158
Nazarite vow   51
NEW AMERICAN BIBLE   14 - 16, 18, 39 - 40, 44 - 45, 48, 70, 73 - 75, 162, 165, 174
NEW YORK TIMES   160
Nicene Council/Conference   59, 79, 81
Nicene Creed   60, 81 - 84
Nineham, D.   59
nineteen   111, 114, 118 - 119, 121 - 125
Numbers
   06:1-21   52
   25:4   13

O
Old Testament   *See:* Torah
Omniscience/Omnipotence
   See : God, qualities of

Origen   169

P
Paraclete   178
Paradise   156, 169
Paul   6, 19, 37, 39, 51, 53 - 57, 60, 64, 68, 74
   epistles of   6, 18 - 19, 37, 39 - 40, 55, 60, 71, 154
Peale, N. V.   98
Peter   144, 158, 165, 187
Philippians
   2:14-15   72
   2:5-7   39
pilgrimage   191
prayer   30, 94, 110 - 113, 190
pre-existence   46 - 47
Presbyterian Church   2
Proverbs
   8:22-23   38
   8:22-26   46
   8:33-36   38
Psalm
   08:4-5   96, 100
   08:5   65
   14:1-3   116
   16:7-9   106
   19:2-5   104
   30:7-8   107
   33:13-15   105
   33:6-9   104
   68:33-35   101
   80:18   66
   89:06-7   77
   89:07   67

89:27-28 67
91:1-13 92
113:4-6 107

Q

Qumran 57
Quran 24, 36, 76, 84, 89, 101, 114 - 115, 117 - 125, 127 - 129, 135, 141, 145, 154 - 156, 170, 173-174, 178-184, 186, 188-192
02:154 157
02:24-26 191
02:25 156
02:261 191
02:285 177
02:29 102
02:62 188
03:169 156
03:35-37 127
03:37-38 132
03:42 128
03:45 36, 134, 174
03:45-47 129
03:48-49 142
03:49 115, 142, 145, 148
03:50-51 176
03:54-55 157
03:59 37, 133
03:81 47
04:157-158 155, 161
04:171 134
04:80 41
05:109 170
05:110 25, 115, 142, 145, 147
05:112-115 148

05:116-119 171
05:44 179
05:46 179
05:48 179
05:69 188
05:72-76 85
06:103 107
06:59 106
07:104-108 139
07:143 180
07:172 47
07:172-174 189
10:61 106
10:62-64 182
11:1-2 42
11:73 132
14:48 170
15:28-29 134, 142
19:16-22 129
19:23-36 131
19:27-30 142
19:27-33 173
19:27-34 24
19:30-34 109
19:34 115
19:88-96 76
21:19-24 181
21:91 134, 176
24:55 182
26:60-66 140
32:17 192
33:72 184
34:25 89
36:26-27 157
39:67 102
39:68 171

39:68-69   169
47:15   191
53:38-39   89
53:43,48   107
59:22-24   108
65:10-11   42
67:3   101
112:1-4   108
Quranic initials   118, 122 - 124

R
religion, contradictions in   96
responsibility, personal   88 - 89
resurrection   156
   day of   156, 169 - 171, 189
   See also: Jesus, resurrection of
Revelation
   01:1-2   25
   1:8   45
   21:1   170
Richardson, C.C.   50
Robber Council   82
Romans   40
   01:03-4   75
   08:14   65, 177
   08:14-21   69
   08:28-29   71

S
Sadler, T.W.   115
Sagan, C.   20
Samarians   148
Samaritans   90, 174, 190
2 Samuel
   22:1-3   89

Satan   93 - 94, 137, 180 - 183, 185 - 187, 189 - 190, 192
Saul of Tarsus   *See:* Paul
Savior   *See:* God as; or Jesus as
Schaberg, J.   126
Schroeder, W. J.   160 - 161
SCIENTIFIC AMERICAN   118
scripture, as messenger   42
Shane, D.   100
Sirach
   15:14-16   88
   16:12-14   88
   22:27-23:1   66
   51:10   66
solar system   99 - 100, 115
Solomon   47
Son of Man
   See: Jesus, as Son of Man
Sonship to God   66 - 72, 76 - 77, 83, 91, 94 - 95, 177, 185, 188
soul   155, 157, 159, 186, 188, 190 - 191
STRONG'S EXHAUSTIVE CONCORDANCE   90
suffering   95
   as admission test   93
   cause of   91
   not for God's children   91 - 92
Super-Apostles   *See:* Apostles

T
Taylor, V.   65, 69, 90, 135
testing of human being   93 - 94
Theodore the Studite   61
Theodotus of Byzantium   79

1 Timothy
   03:16   40
Torah   41, 44, 66, 90 - 91, 117, 176, 178 - 179
translation problems   12, 14 - 16, 21, 39, 74
Trinity   32, 59, 61, 63, 78 - 86, 109, 134, 172

U
Unitarians   85
Unity   85
universes   99 - 102, 107, 181

V
Virgin birth   65, 126 - 136, 141, 172

W
WASHINGTON POST   160
Wells, G.A.   3
Wiles, M.   59
Wilken, R. L.   6, 52, 82
Wirtanen, C.   100
Wisdom personified   37 - 38, 46
Word of God   35 - 36, 41 - 42, 73, 82, 133 - 134
'worship'   13, 15

Y
Yates, J.   78
Young, F.   59 - 60

Z
Zachariah   127, 132

UNIVERSAL UNITY

When we examine the history of mankind we know that the descendants of Adam have one thing in common—God, the Creator. What is dividing us? The human factors in our religions. If we can concentrate on the message that all the messengers brought to humanity, then our problem is solved. All the messengers brought only one message—to worship God alone. Therefore, let us keep our focus on God, and God alone. Hence, Universal Unity has been formed.

OTHER PUBLICATIONS AVAILABLE

THE TIMES OF UNIVERSAL UNITY. Bimonthly news bulletin of Universal Unity. Wide range of fascinating articles discussing and demonstrating the principles of Universal Unity. Something for the whole family. $6.00. Annual Subscription.

QURAN: The Final Testament. Revised edition. Translated by Rashad Khalifa, Universal Unity, 1992. Authorized English version. Clear, powerful, modern English. 536 pages. $7.95. ISBN 0-9623622-2-0.

UNIVERSAL UNITY
P.O. Box 15067, Fremont, CA 94539

BEYOND PROBABILITY: God's Message in Mathematics. By Abdullah Arik, Monotheist Productions, Tucson, AZ, 1992. *Series One: The Opening Statement of the Quran.* 40 pages. $1.90 plus postage.

THE MONOTHEIST NEWSLETTER. Newsletter of Monotheist Productions. Focuing on the continuing discoveries of new mathematical miracles within the Quran. Exciting history as it is made.

INTERNATIONAL COMMUNITY OF SUBMITTERS
P.O. Box 43476, Tucson, AZ 85733-3476